Native Nostalgia

Native Nostalgia

by
Jacob Dlamini

To Evelinah Papayi

First published by Jacana Media (Pty) Ltd in 2009
First impression 2009
Second impression 2010

10 Orange Street
Sunnyside
Auckland Park 2092
South Africa
+2711 628 3200
www.jacana.co.za

© Jacob Dlamini, 2009

All rights reserved.

ISBN 978-1-77009-755-1

Set in Ehrhardt 12/16pt
Job No. 001399

See a complete list of Jacana titles at www.jacana.co.za

Contents

Introduction 1
1 Sounds on the Air. 25
2 Township in Sight. 43
3 Strangers from Underground 65
4 Class Warfare 77
5 The Texture of Money 95
6 The Sense of Township Life. 115
7 The Language of Nostalgia 135
8 Conclusion 151
References 165

Introduction

In August 2009 I travelled to Thandukukhanya, a township in the border town of Piet Retief, about 300 kilometres southeast of Johannesburg, to speak to residents about violent protests that had taken place in the area two months earlier. The protests, against shoddy service delivery by the local municipality, were not unique to the area. In fact, they had become the staple of political life in many parts of South Africa as communities pressed their claims on government agencies buckling under the pressure of ever-growing public demands and expectations, incompetence and corruption. However, Thandukukhanya's protests were unique in at least two respects. Where the average protest drew from the repertoire of the 'politics of the spectacle' that defined direct action in South Africa – the revelry, the burning down of government property, the erection of petrol-soaked tyre barricades and the inevitable handover of a memorandum of demands to a government official – it rarely resulted in death. Thandukukhanya's protests were both spectacular and violent. They claimed three lives, including that of a 71-year-old grandmother. Secondly, Thandukukhanya was the first township to go out in protest following the election of Jacob Zuma in April 2009 as South Africa's fourth democratically elected president. For pundits who had seen in Zuma's election a populist take-over of the ruling African National Congress (ANC) from the allegedly aloof Thabo Mbeki, news of the first protests (not to mention their violent nature) under Zuma's watch came as a surprise.

My trip to Thandukukhanya was part of a research project into the causes of collective violence in service delivery protests, labour strikes and expressions of xenophobia in South Africa. A colleague and I interviewed about a hundred residents, from activists, councillors and priests to the police. Among those we interviewed was an 84-year-old resident of the township. Mrs Pamase Violet Nkabinde was the archetypal pillar of the community. A former school teacher and principal who could honestly claim to know every old family in Thandukukhanya and to have taught anyone who was anyone in this small township, Mrs Nkabinde had many firsts to her name. She started the township's first day-care centre and founded Thandukukhanya's only school for people with disabilities (which earned her nomination as a finalist in the *Sowetan* Community Builder of the Year competition in 2001). A grandniece of Pixley ka Isaka Seme, a founder member of the ANC, Mrs Nkabinde served as a community councillor from 1985 to 1990. Except for the three years (1941–1943) she spent training to become a teacher at St Chad's, an Anglican mission school in the old Natal, Mrs Nkabinde had lived all her life in Thandukukhanya. She was, in her words, 'the oldest person in the township'. Asked what caused the protests, Mrs Nkabinde was not lost for explanations. She listed factors ranging from inexperience and corruption to a condescending council. Recalling an incident during which she confronted the municipality three times for billing her R400 for an allegedly leaky tap, Mrs Nkabinde said a municipal officer insisted she must pay because 'the machine says your tap is leaking'. There was no leak. Mrs Nkabinde remarked: 'They [municipal officials] say hurtful things. They talk as if we don't know what kind of animal is a computer.' So it was not surprising to find that Mrs Nkabinde sympathised with the thousands of residents who took to the streets to protest against the municipality. After all, she too had her own grievances against the council. 'All the complaints make sense,' she said. Her support for the protests was not, however, so simple. 'The only thing that worries me is their [the protesters'] actions. To burn down the clinic for us old ladies, with our high blood pressure and [bad] knees … it was a big mistake.' Now pensioners had to either walk to town or fork out R12 in taxi fare for a round trip to a former whites-only clinic or the new hospital in Piet Retief.

According to Mrs Nkabinde, a devout Methodist, Thandukukhanya used to be so religious and peaceful, 'not even '76 touched us'. ('76 is the student uprising that for some marks the beginning of the end of apartheid.) In her younger days, she said, leaders were 'groomed in the church'. They were educated. The local council also had a dog tax, a bicycle tax and a car tax to fill the municipal coffers. 'They [the new municipality that came in with the advent of democracy in the early 1990s] killed these votes [taxes]. It did not occur to them that they would need the revenue,' said Mrs Nkabinde.

Thandukukhanya had become foreign to her. 'I don't know it now. It was a quiet place with no violence. Even when there were grievances, we did not rise up and fight.' Nowadays, she said, 'there is no corner without a shebeen'. But that was not the only sign of a place and time out of joint. Apartheid was founded on white anxieties about the mass movement of Africans into the urban areas: white farmers experienced this as a serious shortage of labour; while white workers and urban residents feared the *oorstroming* (over-running) of white areas by Africans. Though the Nationalists did not invent influx control, they made sure it was tightened when they assumed office in 1948.

Mrs Nkabinde grew up at a time when outsiders could not move into or stay in a township without a government permit. Influx control was harsh. According to Philip Bonner and Noor Nieftagodien, 'Pass law convictions rose 25% in the first year of National Party rule.' But influx control, which ended in the mid-1980s when the Nationalists reformed apartheid, was remembered benignly by Mrs Nkabinde. In her view the problems of today started 'with the influx of people and shacks. Izihambi seziziningikakhulu. There are too many outsiders. I don't even know where they come from.' To be fair to her, Mrs Nkabinde did not say she missed apartheid. But she did miss something of the past.

Across town from Mrs Nkabinde's house, in the formerly white Piet Retief, lived Thembi Ngcobo, a businesswoman who was also a native of Thandukukhanya. Mrs Ngcobo was half Mrs Nkabinde's age but she, too, was nostalgic about the past. She remembered Thandukukhanya as a quiet place. Mrs Ngcobo said that even when the township embarked on a rent boycott in 1986–87, years after many townships around South Africa had stopped paying for municipal services, it went the legal route. The local council had introduced a pay-as-you-earn rental scheme which residents objected to as it penalised those earning more. The case went all the way to the Appeal Court in Bloemfontein. Mrs Ngcobo was also sympathetic to the protesters. Corruption was rife, nepotism endemic and municipal services poor. According to Mrs Ngcobo, the officials and councillors running the municipality, now named Mkhondo after the river, once called Assegai by Afrikaners, that runs along the western boundary of Piet Retief, were interested only in lining their pockets. They did not care about community upliftment. 'The old government was better,' she said. 'They would come to us and report.'

Mrs Ngcobo's sentiments echoed those made by a man named Vincent Ntswayi in a *Time* magazine report published on the eve of South Africa's general elections on 22 April 2009. According to the *Time* correspondent Alex Perry, Mr Ntswayi, 53, lived in Mvezo, the Eastern Cape village in which Nelson Mandela was born. Mr Ntswayi was jobless and disillusioned with the ANC. 'My life was better during apartheid,' said Mr Ntswayi. 'Freedom turned out to be just a word. Real freedom, real power, that comes from money – and I haven't got any money.' There is no reason to doubt either Mr Ntswayi's existence or sincerity, despite the fact that it has become

Native Nostalgia

all too common for enterprising journalists to find, at each election, someone, usually a pensioner or hard-up citizen, to say just how miserable things are today – compared to the past, which was of course plentiful. There are certainly millions of people out there who share the sentiments expressed by Mrs Nkabinde, Mrs Ngcobo and Mr Ntswayi.

For someone long used to hearing debates about South Africa's transition to democracy being couched in stark terms as either a neoliberal capitulation to the market (a tack favoured by sections of the left) or TINA (the 'there is no alternative' mantra beloved of moneyed black and white elites), it is both illuminating and unsettling to hear ordinary South Africans cast their memories of the past in such a nostalgic frame. It is illuminating because it sheds light on 'ordinary' understandings of our past. It is also unsettling because it reveals that South Africans are not agreed on the meaning of their past. If the pass laws were such a hated symbol of apartheid, as many of us think they were, why would Mrs Nkabinde remember them so fondly? The truth is that there are millions of people who think like Mrs Nkabinde. It does not mean that they supported apartheid. In fact, I do not have to go far from my own circles to find feelings similar to the ones expressed by her.

My brother N always complains about the lack of respect for zoning laws and municipal by-laws in Katlehong, our home town: 'Akusenamthetho. Abantu bazenzel' umathanda' (There is no order any more. People do as they please). To hear my brother, 15 years my elder, tell it, Katlehong was a haven of order in his youth. He tells the story of a local policeman

Introduction

who was so revered that he would round up wanted criminals on foot and without the aid of handcuffs or a gun. The man would start his rounds early, going from address to address. At each place, he would order those he had already rounded up to wait for him by the gate. My brother says: 'He would issue one warning to the people arrested: "Don't let me find you gone. You won't like it if I have to look for you a second time."' That, apparently, is all the cop would say. The men would obey like sheep. Having rounded up his lot, the cop would lead them all in single file to the local police station, stopping along the way to greet neighbours and take tea with friends. That, for my brother, was order.

The story echoes a tale related to Jonny Steinberg by Mtutuzeli Matshoba, the Soweto writer. According to Matshoba, there were two kinds of policemen in Soweto when he was growing up in the 1970s. The first were the Blackjacks, municipal police officers who did not carry guns and 'whose main task was to enforce the pass laws'. Here is what Matshoba tells Steinberg: 'It is almost magical how powerful those pass laws were. A blackjack walks in to see your pass, he takes it, puts it in his pocket, and you must follow him. He gathers a few people like this. One cop followed by 12 people. He is on his bicycle, the 12 are jogging to keep up with him. He stops to see this and that one, to drink and to visit, and the 12 wait for him outside. Then he gets on his bicycle again, and the 12 jog again to keep up with him. He has your passbook in his pocket, and you are nothing without it. You cannot *be* without your passbook. You must follow him.'

The stories told by my brother and Matshoba are uncannily

similar. In my brother's telling, the story is about law and order; in Matshoba's mouth, it is about the injustice of the pass laws. However, it is another story in Matshoba's interview with Steinberg that has greater resonance for this book. The story, which concerns the second kind of policeman in the Soweto of Matshoba's childhood, challenges the conventional struggle narrative of apartheid in which resisters stood on one side and collaborators on the other. The story shows that there was a fine line between resistance and collaboration. Sometimes collaborators would become resisters and vice versa. It was never simply a case of resisters on this side and collaborators on the other. Sometimes, the two were one and the same person. The policemen who bring out this contradiction in Matshoba's story were the reservists. They had no police training and their job was to hunt down people without passes. According to Matshoba, the reservists were corrupt and brutal. The most notorious of them was a man named Skosana. 'He and his friends were like hell lions sauntering down the street, sweeping anything that was male. You couldn't talk back. If you did, they would plant a knife on you that they had taken from someone who had bribed them earlier. It was legalised extortion,' said Matshoba.

The reservists prowled the grounds outside the Mzimhlophe railway station, waiting to pounce on men without passes. The Matshobas' house was opposite the station and Matshoba's father despised the reservists. 'My father never allowed them to step foot in his yard. He would pick up a stick and challenge them. He despised them. I learnt that from him. I did the same as him. People fled into our yard from the station and I

Introduction

would keep the reservists out. So they knew me: they knew me as someone whom they must teach a lesson.' One afternoon, Skosana's pride found Matshoba at the station. They searched him, found nothing, but slapped him on the face anyway. Matshoba fought back. Just then, Matshoba's mother and her friends appeared. Matshoba told Steinberg: 'You will not believe what they did. They joined in on the side of the reservists and laid into me with their handbags. "How can you fight the law like that?" my mother shouted. "These men are working for the law. What trouble are you trying to bring?"'

For Steinberg, the meaning of this story is 'slippery, the lessons it teaches complicated and unclear'. Skosana and his fellow predators were thugs and yet Matshoba's mother, a nurse, sided with them in their tussle against her son. 'Why?' Steinberg asks. 'On the one hand, she was acknowledging that these thugs were dangerous, that the state itself was lethally dangerous, that in this world her son ought to keep his head down. And so her anger was maybe the displaced expression of a great fear. But perhaps something else was going on. Mrs Matshoba's son was a young man at a time when many young men were running wild ... It was a time of notorious thuggery, and without a decent police service, there was nothing to keep it in check. So perhaps Mrs Matshoba was expressing a hunger for authority, for men in uniform who would throw a cordon around her son's life to stop him from straying. That she had to invest this wish in the thugs who menaced the Mzimhlophe station platform has about it a feeling of pathos; in this deformed world, order and authority became confused with state violence and depravity.'

Native Nostalgia

The story resonates with me because this is precisely the kind of thing my mother and all the adults in my neighbourhood did. I can picture her using her slippers, quilted belt and hands to smack me for daring to raise my hands against an adult, regardless of who or what that adult was. For me, however, the slippery meaning of Matshoba's story extends beyond the relationship of black people with the state. I won't forget the day my mother belted me for talking back to a curmudgeonly neighbour. My friends and I were playing football in the street when someone, possibly me seeing that I had to retrieve the ball afterwards, kicked the ball into Mr Curmudgeon's garden. It was an accident. But the gentleman did not care. He let rip with his mouth, calling me and my friends names. That did not bother us. We had had enough run-ins with the man to know he was a miserable sod. We would often bow our heads in feigned shame while he held on to our ball and lectured us on what future awaited our sorry asses. Then he would release our ball, kicking it as far as he could. But this time he went too far. He called my mother names and wondered aloud what sort of woman had raised me. I responded by wondering aloud what sort of mother had raised such a miserable man. He did not like that one bit. As he made to chase me down the street, my mother appeared. She demanded to know what was going on. The man promptly told her I had called him names. 'But he called you names first,' I protested to my mother, thinking she would side with me. 'Thula wena!' Shut up, she told me, as she smacked me across the face with a bare hand. Mother apologised to the man and dragged me home, where she proceeded to smack me some more.

Introduction

It did not matter that the man had insulted her honour. The man was older than I was and deserved my respect, regardless of his conduct. 'Wake wabonaphi abantwana balwa nabantu abadala!' asked my mother. 'Where have you seen children fighting with adults?' It took me a while to forgive my mother for what was to my young mind betrayal. As for Mr Curmudgeon, he died a few years later (neighbours said of cancer), still bitter and miserable. Even his wife had long left him by the time he died.

It is tempting to see in my punishment by my mother an illustration of a generational order in which adults were always right and children had no voice. There was certainly an element of that in her anger towards me. She may also have been expressing, like Matshoba's mother, a hunger for order in a world that had, by the 1980s when I was growing up, got more out of joint than during Matshoba's young adult life in the 1970s. As Barrington Moore says, 'for very many human beings, especially the mass of human beings at the bottom of the pyramid in stratified societies, social order is a good thing in its own right, one for which they will often sacrifice other values'. Looking back on my mother's actions, I find I have today an understanding, a generosity of spirit perhaps, that I did not have as a stubborn 12-year-old. It is this spirit that makes me want to take seriously the nostalgic claims about the past made by Mrs Nkabinde, Mrs Ngcobo, Mr Ntswayi and, of course, my brother.

It would be easy to bend the sentiments expressed by these men and women to our ideological liking. To the leftists who refuse to accept that there is a difference between apartheid and the current order, these sentiments might serve as proof of just how *vrot* things are. To our revolutionaries-turned-rulers, these nostalgic feelings might be nothing more than the musings of reactionaries and even apologists for apartheid. Far more difficult, I think, would be to take seriously these sentiments as one possible way through which we can understand the past and contemporary South Africa. The sentiments confirm that people's lives have changed – though not in the way often imagined. It is all too often taken for granted that the story of black South Africa is one long romance, starting in some golden age during which Africans lived in harmony with the land and each other, followed by the trials and tribulations of European conquest, segregation and apartheid, and ending in triumph with Nelson Mandela, the romantic figure par excellence, taking the military salute as South Africa's first democratically elected leader. In this romantic telling, there is a neat separation between a merry precolonial Africa, a miserable apartheid South Africa and a marvellous new South Africa in which everyone is living democratically ever after. That, alas, is not so. There are many South Africans for whom the past, the present and the future are not discrete wholes, with clear splits between them.

These are people for whom the present is not the land of milk and honey, the past not one vast desert of doom and gloom, and the ancient past not one happy-go-lucky era. For many, the past is a bit of this, the present a bit of that and the future hopefully a mix of this, that and more. For these people, among whom I count myself, there is a conundrum that cannot be got rid of easily by the lazy evocation of labels

Introduction

such as 'sell-outs' or 'self-hating blacks'. The conundrum is this: What does it mean for a black South African to remember life under apartheid with fondness? What does it mean to say that black life under apartheid was not all doom and gloom and that there was a lot of which black South Africans could be, and indeed were, proud? Only lazy thinkers would take these questions to mean support for apartheid. They do not. Apartheid was without virtue.

To understand the question of what it means for a black South African to remember his life under apartheid with fondness is to appreciate that the freedom of black South Africans did not come courtesy of a liberation movement. There were bonds of reciprocity and mutual obligation, social capital, that made it possible for millions to imagine a world without apartheid. To apply what E.P. Thompson said of the English working class, black South Africans were present at their making as citizens. Freedom was not sent to them in a gift box from Lusaka. At the same time, this is not to say that every black South African was against apartheid. That would be a lie.

Apartheid meant, as Steinberg says, a 'deformed world' in which 'order and authority became confused with state violence and depravity'. But that does not mean black life under apartheid sank into a moral void. People knew the difference between right and wrong. They might not have always acted the 'right' way. But they knew their actions constituted a moral choice. This is not to say glibly that power implicates in its exercise those over whom it is exercised. It is to say rather that my mother still believed in respect for elders

Native Nostalgia

even in a 'deformed' world. To make the point another way, it is to say with Lewis Nkosi that not everything people did was a response to apartheid. At the same time this does not mean that moral agency and a hunger for order were not without their pitfalls.

Take Joe Mamasela, an apartheid assassin who has confessed to at least forty murders he committed as part of a security police death squad. A megalomaniac of note, Mamasela has been known to cloak himself in heroic garb and to treat the ambivalence of black South Africans about their lives under apartheid as justification for his actions. He told the writer Antjie Krog: 'I am happy because the majority of the black people today, even those who were against me, are beginning to get back their senses and ask intelligent questions and they don't get answers.' The 'intelligent questions' Mamasela believes blacks are asking today concern the 'moral purity' of the struggle for freedom. 'Don't think everybody on Robben Island was holy,' Mamasela said to Krog. Some were apartheid spies, 'so not all of them are Jesus Christs, not all of them are Moses as they claim'.

Mamasela might consider his actions legitimate. However, that does not mean ordinary South Africans should be cowed from asking if the men and women who led the struggle were the heroes and heroines of legend. We should not be stopped from asking questions about our past because the likes of Mamasela might be asking similar questions. To be nostalgic for a life lived under apartheid is not to yearn for the depravity visited on South Africa by the likes of Mamasela. It is to yearn, instead, for order in an uncertain world. The question of what it means for blacks to remember their lives under apartheid with fondness does not disappear because Mamasela remembers his criminal past fondly.

In a real sense, to fasten on Mamasela as the embodiment of the kind of moral trap one risks falling into by asking what it means to remember life under apartheid fondly, is to focus on only one version of apartheid. In fact, there were many sides to apartheid: some petty, many structural and, therefore, embedded in social relations. Their effects are still with us. For many black South Africans, apartheid was landlessness, the random pass raids, the daily humiliations of being bumped off a pavement by a white person or having a white person cut in front of you in a queue in a shop. It was also the indignity of paltry wages. Mamasela represents the spectacular side of apartheid. He represents police brutality, government death squads and state graft. But that, as we know, was only one aspect of apartheid. The truth is that the majority of black South Africans did not experience apartheid in its spectacular form.

ⵔⵔⵔ

Why nostalgia?

The future of nostalgia is not, so the joke goes, what it used to be. Neither, I would add, is the past of nostalgia what it used to be. The condition, conventionally understood as a 'longing for a home that no longer exists or has never existed', is no longer what it was when the term was first coined by the Swiss doctor Johannes Hofer in 1688. Using two Greek roots, *nostos* (return home) and *algia* (longing), Hofer 'believed that it was possible 'from the force of the sound Nostalgia to define the sad mood originating from the desire for return to one's native land'. As Svetlana Boym points out in her book *The Future of Nostalgia*, Hofer meant his coinage to diagnose groups such as Swiss mercenaries, students studying away from home and domestic servants working abroad. Symptoms of nostalgia ranged from the ability to see and hear ghosts, a 'lifeless and haggard countenance', nausea, loss of appetite, brain inflammation and cardiac arrest, to a high fever. Sufferers were also prone to suicide. The good news was that the disease could be cured. 'Leeches, warm hypnotic emulsions, opium and a return to the Alps usually soothed the symptoms,' writes Boym. That was in the seventeenth century.

Today, nostalgia, 'a sentiment of loss and displacement', is an incurable condition of modernity. As Boym says, 'It would not occur to us to demand a prescription for nostalgia.' However, the irony about nostalgia is that, for all its fixation with the past, it is essentially about the present. It is about present anxieties refracted through the prism of the past. As Boym and scholars such as Fred Davis point out, it is usually when people feel themselves adrift in a world seemingly out of control that they come down with nostalgia. In some ways, it is because the world has become, as the cliché has it, a global village that we have seen a worldwide boom in 'longing for continuity in a fragmented world'.

The trouble with nostalgia, however, is that it is 'something of a bad word, an affectionate insult at best'. Worse if the word is uttered in the same breath as the term apartheid, I would

Introduction

say. But there is a way out for nostalgics such as me. Nostalgia does not have to be a reactionary sentiment. It does not have to be a hankering after the past and a rejection of the present and the future. There is a way to be nostalgic about the past without forgetting that the struggle against apartheid was just. In fact, to be nostalgic is to remember the social orders and networks of solidarity that made the struggle possible in the first place. Boym has proposed two types of nostalgia as a way of treating what is understood by many to be an incurable condition. The two types are not, she says, 'absolute types, but rather tendencies, ways of giving shape and meaning to longing'. The two are restorative nostalgia and reflective nostalgia. Boym says: 'Restorative nostalgia puts emphasis on *nostos* and proposes to rebuild the lost home and patch up the memory gaps. Reflective nostalgia dwells in *algia*, in longing and loss, the imperfect process of remembrance.' According to Boym, 'The first category of nostalgics do not think of themselves as nostalgic; they believe that their project is about truth.' That, I believe, would define Mamasela. According to Mamasela, only he knows the truth about the past, about which ANC leader was 'genuine' and which one a traitor. As Krog writes: 'Sometimes he [Mamasela] wishes that he had the power of Samson to bring down the castle of the ANC. But the only thing he hopes for now is that his children and his people will know the truth about him.' Now a born-again Christian, Mamasela must believe that the truth shall set him free.

Reflective nostalgia, for its part, 'lingers on ruins, the patina of time and history, in the dreams of another place and another

17

time'. I would add that reflective nostalgia does not take the past for granted. It does not even seek to monumentalise it. Not all freedom fighters were noble individuals deserving of monuments. For reflective nostalgics, there is no monumental past to recreate. Boym says that 'reflective nostalgia cherishes shattered fragments of memory and temporalises space. Restorative nostalgia takes itself dead seriously. Reflective nostalgia, on the other hand, can be ironic and humorous. It reveals that longing and critical thinking are not opposed to one another, as affective memories do not absolve one from compassion, judgment or critical reflection.' Boym's union of longing and critical thinking makes reflective nostalgia an attractive narrative frame for the kind of idiosyncratic engagement with the past essayed here.

But if nostalgia is about present anxieties, what exactly are these concerns for me? What is it about the present that makes me cherish shattered fragments of memory? The book should be considered a modest contribution to ongoing attempts to rescue South African history and the telling of it from what Cherryl Walker has correctly identified as the distorting master narrative of black dispossession that dominates the historiography of the struggle. The master narrative would have us believe that black South Africans, who populate struggle jargon mostly as faceless 'masses of our people', experienced apartheid the same way, suffered the same way and fought the same way against apartheid. That is untrue. Black South African life is as shot through with gender, class, ethnic, age and regional differences (to name only the most obvious distinctions) as life anywhere else in the world.

Introduction

The master narrative blinds us to a richness, a complexity of life among black South Africans, that not even colonialism and apartheid at their worst could destroy. I do not mean that my feelings of nostalgia should be understood the same way that the black pensioner trotted out by newspapers at each general election in South Africa says: 'Things were better under apartheid.' However, as my treatment of Mrs Nkabinde, Mr Ntswayi and the others shows, I am not glib about such sentiments. I challenge facile accounts of black life under apartheid that paint the forty-six years in which the system existed as one vast moral desert, with no social orders, and as if blacks produced no art, literature or music, bore no morally upstanding children or, at the very least, children who knew the difference between right and wrong – even if those children did not grow up to make the 'right' moral choices in their lives.

This is not to say there was no poverty, crime or moral degradation. There was. But none of this determined the shape of black life in its totality. Our family did not have electricity for the first eleven years of my life, but this did not mark my life as dim or lacking in any way. I still had a happy childhood. I do not mean to suggest that all black families were happy in the same way. Each family was, of course, unhappy in its own way. The differences between black families extended beyond questions of domestic bliss and strife. There were class, ethnic and gender differences aplenty. It behoves any history worthy of the name to take these differences seriously, which could be as small as the type of lawn one had in one's yard, the type of furniture in each bedroom, or the kind of fencing one had around the yard – whether it was the concrete slabs called 'stop nonsense' or the wire mesh fence we had around our house. These differences spoke of everything and nothing at the same time – such as the fact that some families had money and others did not.

There are also immediate anxieties at the heart of my nostalgia. I am concerned that in its technocratic drive to erase the legacies of apartheid and to bring about economic development, the ANC has created an anti-politics machine in which black people – who allegedly suffered the same way, struggled the same way and lived the same way under apartheid – feature as nothing more than objects of state policies or, worse, passive recipients of state-led service delivery.

But, as the residents of Thandukukhanya showed in June 2009 when they burnt down government property, don't assume that if you build a clinic they will attend it. More likely they will burn it down, especially if its shelves are forever empty because some state official has pocketed the money intended for essential medicines and the nurses on duty are surly sisters more adept at insulting patients than at providing primary care. Don't assume that if you build a library, residents should be forever grateful to you. Not when they are paying for such services and definitely not when their votes have given your party solid majorities for the past fifteen years.

In fact, the anti-politics machine of the ANC has succeeded only in breeding political entrepreneurs and racial nativists. For this lot, there are no local histories, no differences within black South Africa. We are all the same to them. When I asked an official of the Ekurhuleni Metropolitan Council in 2006

Introduction

for access to the archives of the old Germiston and Katlehong municipal councils, the official asked why. Oh, because I am writing a book about Katlehong, I said. 'But, bro, Katlehong doesn't exist any more. Why don't you write a book about Ekurhuleni instead,' he said.

Ekurhuleni did not exist until 2000, when the ANC effected nationwide local government reform that resulted in the amalgamation of formerly white and black municipalities. Katlehong was established in 1949. Still, this attempt at distorting history is, to my mind, the lesser of the many evils made possible by the corruption of black history we see all around. Far more dangerous is what has been made possible by the fiction that black South Africans lived, suffered and struggled the same way against apartheid. This has allowed racial nativists to claim with impunity that if all blacks suffered the same way, then any black person can stand in for all blacks. It has made it all too easy for some to play the race card. It has also allowed a few black faces to get rich at the expense of millions of blacks – all in the name of black economic empowerment and transformation, whatever that means.

There is perhaps no uglier example of this than the case of John Hlophe, the judge president of the Western Cape. If playing the race card were professional poker, Hlophe would be rich. Here is a man with no struggle history to speak of accusing heroes and heroines of the struggle of being anti-transformation. Today, he is being punted by his fellow racial nativists as the man to bring about judicial transformation. All because he is black.

We often joke that there is not a single white South African today who will admit to having supported apartheid. As Hannah Arendt says, when all are victims, then no one is a victim. The time has come to tell a similar joke about all these black folks suddenly claiming that they, too, were freedom fighters. They must be caught out with their lies. These, then, are some of the anxieties and concerns that animate this book. They are by no means the only preoccupations here. I am also keen to tell stories about the Katlehong of my childhood.

What follows are fragments, shards of memory through which I examine indirectly what it means to be nostalgic for a past generally considered to have been a dark chapter in South Africa's history. I use fragments drawn randomly from the past to look at my childhood in Katlehong as a lived experience. How might one relay the history of Katlehong in terms of the senses of smell, hearing, taste, touch and sight? I attempt to answer that question. I look at how black schools, intended by the government to be a great downward leveller of black ambition, played on ideas of contamination and senses of sound and smell to heighten class consciousness within black society, often pitting the local elite against the 'mass' of the great black unwashed. I also use my sensory experience of Katlehong to examine the place of radio in the life of an urban black family in apartheid South Africa. Here, I do not simply wish to relay the auditory experience of listening to the radio but to look, rather, at how the very instrument (the radio) that was supposed to be the government's propaganda tool actually had the opposite effect, awakening in me a political consciousness that saw me adopt a politics at odds with the political gradualism and religious conservatism of my mother.

Introduction

The book will have succeeded if it helps the reader come to a new sense of townships, to develop a different kind of common sense about them. I won't prescribe how this book should be read. As one erudite Frenchman put it, the death of the author comes the moment a reader picks up a book.

1

Sounds on the Air

Save yo drama for yo Mama
– Message on a bumper sticker

To the Chinese, it was the year of the Ox; to the Soviets, the year they said *nyet* to the broadcast of the imperialist *Sesame Street* on Soviet television; to the Germans, the year both East and West were admitted to the United Nations; to the Israelis, the year they won the Yom Kippur War; to the Brits, the year car owners scrambled to fill up as government introduced fuel rationing; to the Americans, the year the Supreme Court legalised abortion with its decision in *Roe* v. *Wade*; and to Evelinah Papayi Dlamini, a 45-year-old working-class woman from Katlehong, a black township about 30 kilometres east of Johannesburg, the year her only surviving child was born. I was born on a Monday in Natalspruit Hospital, a 900-bed edifice since condemned to demolition for lying on dolomitic ground, on 29 January 1973. To be fair to my mother, she would not share any of the melodrama of this passage. In fact, save for the oil crisis of that year, whose inflationary effects were felt the world over, it is doubtful she would have paid any attention to things such as the Chinese calendar.

Native Nostalgia

She probably followed the news about the Soviets, Germany and the Yom Kippur War on the wireless. The radio is also where, if she cared for such things, she would have heard in the year I was born that in the US, *Angie* by the Rolling Stones, *Brother Louie* by Stories, *Crocodile Rock* by Elton John, *Love Train* by the O'Jays and *Let's Get It On* by Marvin Gaye were the hits of the year. She would have known that in South African townships, blacks were grooving to the mbaqanga of Mahlathini and the Mahotella Queens, the isicathamiya of Ladysmith Black Mambazo, the township soul of Mpharanyana and the Cannibals, and, of course, the soul of the O'Jays and Marvin Gaye. The eldest in a family of ten, my mother was the daughter of a Sotho-speaking farm-hand and a Zulu-speaking domestic. She was a woman of modest schooling and little interest in Western popular music – except gospel, mbaqanga, isicathamiya (which two of her brothers sang) and the crooning of Jim Reeves, the Texan folk singer who toured South Africa in the early 1960s, recorded songs in Afrikaans and starred in a movie set in South Africa.

In American cinemas, the Academy Award winner *The Sting*, *The Exorcist*, *American Graffiti*, *Papillon*, *Live and Let Die*, and *Mean Streets* were some of the best movies of the year. On American TV, *Kojak*, *M*A*S*H* and *The Waltons* were the television favourites. Not that South Africans would have known any of this. South Africa did not have television until 1976. It is said that the Protestants who ran apartheid South Africa did not trust television. These men feared that television would corrupt white South Africans and give blacks ideas about freedom and suchlike. They found the TV medium

Sounds on the Air

too egalitarian, too democratic in its orientation for their liking. They were probably right, if one considers that when *The Cosby Show* came to South Africa in the 1980s, the Huxtables became white South Africa's most favourite television family for the better part of the decade. That the fathers of the nation finally relented and allowed television, albeit segregated TV, was due largely to the increasing assertiveness of a growing and confident Afrikaner middle class that wanted it all: good jobs, universities, overseas travel, international sports and big houses complete with swimming pools, armies of servants and, of course, television sets in their living rooms. It was not so much a question of keeping up with the Joneses as it was a matter of being in the global world. For the rulers of South Africa, which had experienced a growth rate in the 1960s second only to Japan's, their Luddite ways must have seemed more ridiculous by the day, especially in the light of their claims to be the last defenders of 'western civilisation' in Africa. They could not exactly claim to be defenders of such civilisation and yet be opposed to television. Something had to give. So they caved in in 1976 and allowed television to come to South Africa. I was of course too young to know any of this at the time. But the absence of television did have its benefits. It meant I was brought up in a world of radio or, as we called it at home, the wireless.

It also meant that I grew up in a family where the imagination was allowed to wander and to dream as we gave body, colour, demeanour and setting to the hundreds of voices that came into our house through the air each day. Deprived sight of the images that were the staple of television, we could see things with our minds unencumbered by the limited medium of television. We befriended the voices of our radio presenters, developing such intimate knowledge of their 'timbre, range, turn of phrase and key words used' that we could identify these voices and their owners even in our sleep. We could, thanks to the wireless, let our imaginations wander. We could see far and wide. We could also be present in places thousands of miles away from Katlehong.

One such place was Akron, the American home town of one Michael Dokes in the Midwestern state of Ohio. The date was 23 September 1983 and Dokes, boxing world heavyweight champion at the time, was defending a title he had won in December 1982. Dokes's challenger was Gerhardus Christiaan Coetzee, a South African fighter with little in the way of stamina but a powerful right hand. Dokes was a black American; Coetzee a white African. Coetzee had already lost to Mike Weaver and John Tate, two big-hitting American boxers, and was not expected to trouble Dokes. But he was South African and a homeboy, coming as he did from the East Rand city of Boksburg, about 10 kilometres from Katlehong. In fact, his nickname was the Boksburg Bomber. Coetzee was an Afrikaner and spoke with a thick Afrikaans accent but he had endeared himself to black South Africans by declaring publicly that he was opposed to apartheid and was no bigot.

My family supported Coetzee and my mother would let me stay up to follow his fights on the radio each time the man went into the ring. He was one of ours and we cheered him on without reservation. We followed every twist and turn of his fight against Dokes, every blow on the radio. As I recall, the fight began promisingly for Dokes. He was quicker than Coetzee and had a bigger arsenal than Coetzee. But he did not look like a man who had trained seriously for this fight. So it did not come as a surprise when, in the fifth round, Coetzee caught Dokes in the jaw with a right hand. The punch sent the champion to the canvas on one knee. But it was not over yet. Coetzee, who had done well not to show his legendary lack of stamina, caught Dokes again in the tenth round. This time Dokes did not get up. The fight was over and the world had a new boxing heavyweight champion. My family was ecstatic. So were the other families in our street. We had all been cheering Coetzee and had all followed the fight on the radio.

Coetzee's victory made him the first African ever to be crowned world heavyweight champion. But the significance of the fight, dubbed the Upset of the Year for 1983 by *KO Magazine*, extended beyond Coetzee's African origins. He also happened to be the first white boxer in twenty-three years to be crowned world heavyweight champion. The world had not had a white world heavyweight champ since 1960 when Ingemar Johansson defeated Floyd Patterson. Given that the sport of boxing is always nursing 'white hopes', I have no doubt there were white supremacists out there who found cynical vindication in Coetzee's triumph. The apartheid South African government must also have tried to milk Coetzee's victory for all it was worth. This was in the early 1980s and the anti-apartheid movement was starting to gain traction and the cultural and sports boycott of South Africa was increasingly becoming noticeable.

We did not care. A better fighter had won on the night.

What's more, the winner was one of us, a South African and a homeboy. That is what mattered. It also helped that Coetzee had used his position as a public figure to speak out against apartheid. Was his opposition to apartheid genuine? After all, his promoter was one Don King, the father of cynicism. It did not matter. What mattered was that Coetzee came from our neck of the woods and was only too happy to advertise the fact. My neighbourhood friends and I followed his fight over the radio and because we could only see with our minds, we embellished every possible detail in our re-enactments the following day. Some took the role of Dokes; others assumed the triumphant poses of the Boksburg Bomber, ducking and weaving as they imagined themselves in that ring thousands of miles away in Akron, Ohio.

News that there were black families that supported Coetzee enthusiastically, and that we would stay up all night or get up early in the morning to follow the broadcasts of his fights on radio, may come as a surprise to those who would like to think that the world of apartheid was one of moral clarity. It might even come as a shock for these people to discover that apartheid South Africa, even at its worst, was never a world of black and white. There were shades of grey, zones of ambiguity that individuals traversed daily as they went about their lives. Naturally, these shades of grey and zones of ambiguity were not experienced the same way. In the case of Coetzee, it may have helped that he was openly opposed to apartheid. But Coetzee was no freedom fighter, no knight in shining armour. He was simply a boxer of moderate talent who got far. None of that mattered, however. What mattered was that he was one

Sounds on the Air

of us and we claimed him as such.

It is also possible that Coetzee's acceptance in our street was helped by the way he was presented by Radio Zulu. For all of this, our deep love for him and the recording of his exploits, was done in Zulu. In fact, Radio Zulu was famous for its sports broadcasts. People who did not speak Zulu as their first language would tune in to the station to follow its broadcasts. This is worth recalling because it went against apartheid communications policy, which sought to connect so-called Bantu radio stations to the doctrine of separate development. In terms of apartheid thinking, these stations sought to promote ethnic consciousness and pride in one's languages. But things did not go according to plan for apartheid's planners.

According to Liz Gunner, the cross-ethnic appeal of supposedly ethnic radio stations was not the only way in which apartheid was undermined. Radio produced a 'socioscape that provided a thick sense of the varieties of place'. Radio also helped create an imagined community in which, as Gunner says, listeners were bound together 'beyond the reach of any ethnic programmer'. However, it was radio's effect on the apartheid conception of space that had the most positive benefit for black South Africans. In a political time and space that was coded in racial terms, with severe limits imposed on black mobility, black people could move through radio in ways that the apartheid state could not curtail. Black people could enjoy a freedom of movement and being that the apartheid regime could not take away. Sure, apartheid censors could limit what one listened to, they could try to dictate what made the news. But they could not determine how the listening public received the propaganda. They could not tell blacks how to listen.

Speaking of Radio Zulu's famous sports presenters and their reports, Gunner says: 'One did not need a pass, or money for travel through apartheid-mapped cities, to move in the mind to that pitch, spurred on by the fevered eloquence and soaring voice of Thetha Masombuka as he created verbal pictures of skill, daring energy, spectacular tries, near misses, penalties, fouls, offsides …' The SABC, out of which came the broadcasts of soccer matches and events such as Coetzee's triumph, was, as Gunner says, 'a heavily racially stratified and racially hierarchical organisation with African-language radio securely (or so it seemed) in the hands of the architects of apartheid and their acolytes'.

In truth, radio in South Africa predated apartheid by at least two decades. The first broadcast was in 1924 and was a private venture. The state did not assume control until 1936 and in fact some of the earliest Zulu broadcasts were in the mid-1920s, with the broadcasting of the performances of the Zulu Versatile Company. The first broadcast in Zulu came in April 1941 and was a war news broadcast by King Edward Masinga. But radio had a limited reach and appeal at the time, given that the radio sets of old were expensive and difficult to buy. Again, it was not until the 1960s with the introduction of the FM frequency and the advent of cheap transistor radio sets that many households, including poor ones, could suddenly afford to own a radio set.

Apartheid planners were not blind to the propaganda possibilities opened up by radio. Radio Bantu was launched

Sounds on the Air

in 1960 and in 1969 a government official described the policy of the SABC in the following terms: the state broadcaster would serve national policy, would recognise the diversity of language groups and different nations in South Africa. This was essentially Bantustan-speak adapted to the SABC. The way apartheid planners saw it, Radio Zulu would promote both pride in Zuluness and authentic Zuluness and also encourage support for the bantustan of Zululand. It would be the same with Radio Sotho, Radio Tswana and so on. But that is not necessarily how things turned out. Apartheid planners and censors saw the SABC as an instrument to 'shape and control the mindset of its listeners'. It did not work. Listeners made of the SABC broadcasts they followed what they willed. Though the SABC could dictate the content, it could not determine the content's reception.

For me, the best part about Radio Zulu was its radio dramas. These were, like the sports broadcasts, journeys of the imagination that did not require one to travel. Here is how Gunner describes how many felt about these dramas: 'Just as listeners would cluster in the intimacy of small living-rooms to listen to football – so, too, would the family, sometimes with an uncle or father who had rushed home from work, sit and listen to "amastori" [stories] or "imidlalo yomoya" [plays of the air].' In the case of my family, we did not have an uncle or father rushing home to be with us on time to listen to radio dramas. There were no men in the house. It was my mother, whichever sister was staying with her at the time, and us children. Come the time of the drama, the children would already have had their evening baths, supper would have been served and we would all be clustered next to the radio in our kitchen, listening to the drama. Our trusted yellow-coloured Defy coal stove would be on, keeping the room warm.

The kitchen would be quiet as we followed the twists and turns of the drama. After the 30-minute-long drama the family would play a game of cards. Occasionally, Aunt Z, who had grown up playing the harmonica in rural Zululand, would whip out her instrument and play it for us. Though we each had our own harmonica, none of us got to play it as well as Aunt Z did, especially the Zulu tunes that made the instrument 'speak' Zulu. The least favourite part of the evening for the children was that we had to take turns washing dishes. That was the family ritual. If my mother had to miss an episode of the radio drama for some reason (say a community meeting or a death in the neighbourhood), the children would be expected to give her a blow-by-blow account of the evening's story. I don't know if this turned us into storytellers but it sure helped improve our powers of concentration.

According to Gunner, some critics have put down the radio dramas as 'an attempt to validate a state of timeless, pastoral Africa, and to underwrite the assumption of the dominant ideology that Africans ... had no place in the city except as brief sojourners'. There is certainly an element of truth in the claim that many of the dramas we followed so keenly traded in the well-worn idea of an idyllic rural Africa in battle with a corrupt urban Africa. In fact, I can't think of a single drama from my youth where the city or a township had any virtue. At times, you would find village idiots, 'backward-minded' rural people who dealt in witchcraft and suchlike, but they tended to be outcasts who stood out because they sought to undermine the rural idyll being presented by the drama.

However, it would be a mistake to conclude from this that these dramas were reactionary and that they only served to brainwash the millions who followed them. To do so would be to patronise the listeners. It also would be 'far too simplistic a reading', says Gunner. But it would be equally shortsighted to pretend that apartheid planners did not achieve some of their intentions. According to Gunner, 'It would be foolish, however, to argue that all the dramas of the 1970s, that decade of contestatory discourses around South African identities, sidestepped the oppressive and segregationist blueprint of the apartheid mandarins of the SABC.' There were, for example, dramas that sought to highlight the 'dangers' posed by 'communist-influenced terrorists', and these dramas were no less popular for their propaganda. People still enjoyed and followed them.

Gunner also points out that the use of the SABC by the apartheid planners to influence minds did not end with dramas and news bulletins. These planners sought to change Zulu itself, appropriating the language and giving it new words in a desperate bid to make it speak of realities vastly different from what people knew. A good example of this provided by Gunner is the provenance of the following word: *iphekulazikhuni*. I grew up knowing and thinking that this was an 'original' and 'authentic' Zulu word meaning terrorist. It turns out, according to Gunner, that the word was actually coined by the SABC to describe freedom fighters. The word literally means 'what blows over a burning faggot' but was developed to refer to militants, Bolshevists and communists.

Ironically, it was because of words such as *amaphekulazikhuni* (plural for terrorist) that my interest in politics was piqued. Because radio was such a central part of our family experience, we got everything from it, from entertainment to news. So I would always listen to the news bulletins. Often, you would hear that terrorists had been shot somewhere, terrorists had been arrested somewhere, or a terrorist had set off a bomb somewhere. I was intrigued. So I would ask my mother: 'Who or what are these terrorists always getting shot at?' 'Why are they getting shot?' 'How does one become a terrorist?' I do not remember my mother's answers but they cannot have been encouraging. Still, I would not be fobbed off, and slowly I began to understand we were living through a low-intensity war and that we were not getting the full picture on Radio Zulu (this was years before the station changed its name, in keeping with the new South Africa, to Ukhozi FM).

To be honest, some of my growing enlightenment came from Radio Zulu itself. There was, for example, a news reader who would always start his bulletins with the line 'Kwangiphinda kelokho', meaning 'There we go again.' The gentleman would preface every item on the bulletin with the line 'Bathi ngithi' (They say I must say this). 'They say I must say that three terrorists were killed in a shootout with the police yesterday.' The man was a genius. He was funny too. His ironic take on the news was perhaps his means of survival. It was certainly an occasion for mirth each time he came on. For me, things got even better when I was introduced to Radio Freedom, the ANC's banned station, by a friend in primary school in

Sounds on the Air

1985. I forget what we had been talking about but the friend, whose mother was my mother's boss at the local women's hostel, told me I could get the station in the afternoons after school. He gave me the dial and of course I tried it when I got home. I got mostly static and snippets. However, the experience further deepened my appreciation for radio. There was obviously more to the instrument than the lies and whims of the apartheid government. The instrument could be used, as I was discovering, to connect me to a bigger and different world from the one I was used to. Through our radio set, I could follow boxing matches taking place in the US, stories such as the death of singer Marvin Gaye, which made quite an impression on me, and the goings-on at the United Nations. Of Nelson Mandela and other leaders in prison, Radio Zulu hardly ever spoke. But there was a lot of the Zulu nationalist leader Mangosuthu Buthelezi, often railing against faction fighting and imploring his 'subjects' to lay down their arms.

I could identify all the presenters by voice: Cyril 'Kansas City' Mchunu, Bhodloza 'the Little Pig' Nzimande, Samuel Mkhwanazi, Lindiwe Ntuli, Mtholephi Mthimkhulu and Wilson Nkosi. But it was the sports presenters who made the strongest impression: men such as Koos Radebe, Zama Zondo and the legendary Thetha Masombuka. These men filled up one's weekend. Gunner sums it up: 'Often, rapport was built up through listeners recognizing the tone, timbre, inflections of a voice, so that years later, a personality who may now be known for his or her role in television plays, is remembered as a presence active in the voices and the voicing of the culture over many years.'

Native Nostalgia

We were definitely not among the first families to get a TV set in our street. As a result we had to visit neighbours if we wanted to watch our favourite shows. In the early 1980s, many families in our street did not yet have electricity, so people used petrol-driven generators to power their engines. My cousin S and I watched TV in Brother Lucas's house directly in front of ours. The trouble with using generators was that you could run out of petrol in the middle of your favourite show. However, that was not so much fun as watching a soccer match at someone's house. Soccer loyalties run very deep in many townships. People take their attachments seriously. There was a man in the neighbourhood who was a passionate supporter of Orlando Pirates, one of the two biggest soccer teams in South Africa. This was way back in the 1980s when Pirates were a hopeless bunch of losers, especially when playing against their archrivals, Kaizer Chiefs.

The Pirates fan with a TV set charged a nominal amount (a couple of cents) for watching TV in his house. However, he would make us sleep on our tummies on the floor under a big table in his dining room. The TV set was placed against the wall on one end of the table and the man sat at the other end. He would position his feet so that he could kick any Chiefs supporter lying on the floor who was stupid enough to voice his celebration of a goal. Sometimes, the man would get so worked up that he would kick us out midway through the game. In fact, it was after one particularly nasty episode with the man that my mother relented and bought the family a TV set. Now we could watch television whenever we wanted, without worrying about troubling a family just sitting down to dinner.

Sounds on the Air

As I grew older, I also took to listening to radio stations other than Radio Zulu. One particular favourite was Radio 5, a white radio station through which I was introduced to rock and heavy metal – to U2, Prince, Billy Idol, Jon Bon Jovi and Midnight Oil. However, no sooner had I been introduced to Midnight Oil than I heard that they had been banned by the SABC and their songs blacklisted. It turned out the Australian group had decided to donate the proceeds from the sale of their album in South Africa to the banned ANC. It was brilliant, getting white South Africans to give money to the ANC – except it did not last, of course. There were other groups that were banned by the various SABC stations, such as the local group Stimela, one of whose albums was deemed to be anti-state. It was not until the end of apartheid that radio was freed in South Africa and DJs could play pretty much what they wanted.

Thanks to the family rituals centred on our radio set and the love we had for radio dramas and storytelling, I have become a radio man through and through. I find radio to this day far more stimulating and engaging. TV dulls my senses and numbs my body. Though I will happily watch TV, I cannot lose myself in it the way I can in a radio drama, for example. I also find that I can watch TV in my sleep as it were, whereas I need to be alert when listening to radio. Overall, the medium is still more popular than television. But that is only because radio is cheaper than a TV set and, unlike a TV set, does not require a lot of maintenance. However, I worry that radio is not as useful as it was in my childhood. Today I can't bear to listen to Ukhozi FM (the renamed Radio Zulu) for more than

Native Nostalgia

a few minutes. This is because there is more English spoken by the DJs and presenters than is necessary and, worse, the music played is no different from what one finds on a dance station. You still get programmes on politics and community issues but these have become sideshows to the 'real' business of making Ukhozi FM sound like a youth station.

It is as if, having survived apartheid censorship and a lack of imagination, the radio station has found itself with an incurable complex: a complex about being a Zulu-medium station when English has been privileged in democratic South Africa as the language of advancement. There is no reason why there should be so much English on Ukhozi FM. We have more than enough English-medium radio stations in the country. I obviously cannot speak for the millions of South Africans in rural areas and townships who depend on Ukhozi FM for their news, dramas and entertainment. But I wonder what they must make of all these changes. Are they, too, nostalgic for the days when to listen to Radio Zulu was to 'listen against the grain'? Are they nostalgic for a time when you conspired with presenters in the comfort of your kitchen to live a full and happy life, despite the designs of the apartheid planners? A time when we could celebrate the crowning of the world's first white boxing heavyweight champion in twenty years – not because the man was white but because he was one of us, a homeboy, and because Radio Zulu made sure to bring him through the wireless into the comfort of our home? It is possible that some might see in my longing for the Radio Zulu of my childhood an atavistic attachment to Zuluness. That would be wrong. I no more care for my 'Zuluness' than I care

Sounds on the Air

for the fact that I am right-handed.

In some ways, my lament over the demise of Zulu-medium radio is not unique. The death of radio has been announced many times before. In the first decades of the twentieth century, Walter Benjamin was mourning the death of radio, seeing in it the concomitant death of the art of storytelling. In a sense, his lament holds for today. There is little storytelling being done in Katlehong nowadays. So let me move on to tell a story about Katlehong, a place of which I have such fond memories.

2

Township in Sight

What does one see when one reads the township from the air?
– Achille Mbembe

In theory, Katlehong was a scientific township. It was laid out in a grid, with streets that intersected at 90° angles, followed neat curves and ended in T-junctions. It was divided into 32 rectangular sections, each named after a local luminary. There were four main entry points into the township. A railway line, running the length of the township, cut the municipality in half. The streets, on which sat houses of various sizes (from one-, two-, three- and five-roomed houses to, well, big houses) had no names. But each house had a number. The number assigned to our semidetached three-roomed house in Nhlapo Section, close to the administrative hub on the northern edge of the township, was, for a boy learning to count, the easiest combination to memorise: 1-2-3-4. To the question 'Sonny, where do you live?' usually asked by older boys trying to establish if they could molest you without incurring the wrath of an uncle or older brother, I would answer: 1-2-3-4 Nhlapo Section. As my confidence grew, I took to saying 12-34. However, cousin N, seven years my junior, had some trouble with the combination when her turn came to memorise our address. 'Tef-tefi-to,' she would say, no doubt trying to render phonetically what her young ears had picked up from the adults around her.

The grid, so elegant in its simplicity that it is sometimes referred to as a chequerboard, is by far the most common pattern for urban planning in the world and has been favoured by political rulers since the dawn of modern political community. It has an especially rich history in Africa that goes all the way back to ancient Egypt. Ancient Egyptians are said to have used the Nile River as a 'great linear axis running north–south and everything had to run alongside it or at right angles to it, in the direction of the rising and setting sun'. Ancient Egypt was also, if we are to believe the Bible, one of the earliest sites in history for the use of house lettering. Recall how important house markings (and presumably the grid) proved to the liberation of the Israelites from Egyptian bondage. God, having instructed Moses to tell each Israelite household in Egypt to slaughter a lamb on the day that would later become Passover, said: 'Then they are to take some of the blood and put it on the sides and tops of doorframes of the houses where they eat the lambs … The blood will be a sign for you on the houses where you are; and when I see the blood, I will pass over you.' The Egyptians were decimated and the Pharaoh, chastened, let God's people go.

Katlehong's house numbers were not daubed, it should be said, in blood but black paint. But it is not an exaggeration to say that they, too, were intended to give government officials God's-eye view of the township, to make the area legible.

Township in Sight

They were intended to allow government officials to see and read the area from a distance. To say that Katlehong was in theory a scientific township is to say that there was a wide gap between how government, with its bird's-eye view of the place, saw it and how those who lived there experienced it. It is, in other words, to speak of the difference between Katlehong as it existed on paper for the state and Katlehong as it looked from the ground, as seen on a human scale. Residents did not so much undermine the grid as neutralise it with practices such as cutting double laps, shortcuts, through neighbours' properties, and erecting stop-nonsense fences whose efficacy depended not on the fences' height but their acceptance by neighbours. Here, the ground on which people lived and walked was founded not on official decrees but on relationships between neighbours. This does not mean the place existed outside politics, for, as Robert Hughes says, all cities are shaped by politics.

The term 'scientific township' was coined in the late 1940s by government urban planners who reckoned they had found a cheap way to house an African urban population that had ballooned on the back of the Second World War – thanks to a manufacturing boom spurred on by the war and the collapse of the rural economy which had pushed thousands of Africans into the slums of Johannesburg and other major cities. Katlehong, built in 1949 on a farm called Natalspruit bought by the city fathers of the township's white 'parent city', Germiston, and other townships like it were 'scientific' because they were unlike the slums that had preceded them – Sophiatown and Alexandra in the case of Soweto and Tembisa,

Native Nostalgia

Stirtonville in the case of Vosloorus, and Dukathole in the case of Katlehong. Only Alexandra remains of these slums: maze-like, densely populated settlements with no official 'order' to their layout. The new townships, on the other hand, were 'properly' laid out in a grid, had wide open roads and, in some cases, numbers on the roofs that could be read from the sky. The streets followed straight lines and neat curves; each house had a yard and ablution facilities that, even if rudimentary, were still an improvement on the hovels that had come before. To be scientific was to be modern and the new townships were considered by both the government and many urban Africans to be better than the slums that had characterised African urban life since the onset of South Africa's Industrial Revolution, which began with the discovery of diamonds in Kimberley in 1868 and gold on the Reef in 1886.

On streets with no names, neighbourhoods took on the designations of whatever landmarks were present. We lived on the Roman Street or *estrateni saseRoma*, to give it its proper township Zulu name, on account of the Roman Catholic church on our block. The house itself sat on a T-junction and the Roman Street ran along an east–west axis past the small gate that led on to our yard. From the gate, you could run your eyes northwards down the road to Grandma Paulinah's semidetached five-roomed house, about 800 metres away. Grandma's house was considered the seat of the Dlamini clan and, as with our house, was known by all in the family simply by its number: 805 Nhlapo Section. Here the landmarks were two shebeens known by their owners' names: Ka-John, across the street from house 805, and KaMazinyane, a block to the

Township in Sight

east of the house. One uncle, who lived about 5 kilometres to the south of 12-34, took the business of house numbers so seriously that his address became his nickname: 5-5 Zuma Section. 'Here comes Uncle 5-5,' my cousins and I would shout each time we saw him on the street. 'That's right, *bashana*, Uncle 5-5 is here,' he would say. *Bashana* is Zulu for nephews. When Uncle 5-5 died, his nickname devolved on to his widow.

Immediately to the south of us, parallel to the Roman Street, was Embassy Row. Here stood the 'consulates' of Transkei, Ciskei, Qwaqwa and KwaNdebele – four of the eight make-believe homelands to which every urban African was meant to belong, for we were but sojourners in 'white' South Africa, visitors who would return to their tribal enclaves one day. To the east of Embassy Row stood Emabhodweni, the administrative centre of the township, so named because of the three-legged pots that served as flower pots outside the single-storey brick building. Emabhodweni housed the town clerk's office, the rent office, a library and, adjacent to it, the magistrate's courts, and the township's police station and holding cells. To the immediate west of the police station stood the local swimming pool, a beer hall and D.H. Williams Community Hall, named after one of the last white men to manage Katlehong. In front of the hall was the township's only softball diamond. This area, with its many buildings, was the local seat of government and might as well have been, for all that, the centre of Katlehong. But geographically it was not the centre.

In addition to the local seat of government and its various agencies, we also had a post office, a Barclays Bank and a

Native Nostalgia

Standard Bank, for the longest time the only banks in the township. The first time I heard the term 'economic sanctions' used in the township was in the early 1980s when we woke up one day, as it seemed, to discover the local Barclays had been renamed First National Bank. 'Kedi-sanctions [It's the sanctions],' the adults said by way of explanation. Across the street from the post office was a bottle store and, I believe, the biggest news agent in Katlehong. People would gather here, especially on Sunday mornings, to read newspapers, taking turns to share a single edition. The public sphere so created was inspired as much by the need for the males who gathered there to gloat or commiserate over their football teams' performance as it was by economics: very few people could afford to buy a newspaper outright. The news agent's building faced diagonally on to a bus stop and a taxi rank that served both local and outside commuters. From here you could catch a bus or a taxi to anywhere in the township or to the vast beyond that was the world outside Katlehong. To the north of Katlehong stood industrial towns such as Wadeville, with its gigantic Scaw Metals, and Germiston beyond that; to the east of Katlehong stood Vosloorus township and, further east from that, Boksburg; to our west was Alrode with its many chemical plants; to the south, in the great distance, were farmlands that stretched as far as the eye could see towards Heidelberg Hills, part of the Drakensberg escarpment. In keeping with apartheid urban planning, Katlehong was twinned with an Indian township named Palm Ridge to its south and, to the immediate west of Palm Ridge, a coloured neighbourhood called Eden Park. To the north-west of Eden Park was a

Township in Sight

township called Thokoza. Germiston was where you did all your serious shopping – for furniture, clothes and groceries. It was, in the official parlance of the day, our 'white parent city'. Johannesburg Maboneng, the city of lights, was 30 kilometres to the west of us. This, in short, was the world around us, the world to which thousands commuted by train and bus and on foot each weekday morning for work or, as circumstances changed towards the late 1980s, to look for work.

Like every government-built house in Katlehong, ours was made up of concrete slabs and boasted an asbestos roof. This was years before it was discovered that asbestos was toxic. In fact, the asbestos roof was chosen by government planners because it was cheap and, unlike steel, did not rust under the African sun. I have already mentioned our small gate. There was a second gate, for cars, that opened on to an L-shaped lawn that covered the street- and front-side of the house. In front of the house stood a peach tree that I grew up thinking had always been there. I discovered later that the tree had actually come with the house. This was part of government efforts to make townships liveable and conducive to the pursuit of the happy life. Next to the tree, there was a tiny path that led from the stoep in front of the only door to the house all the way to our flush toilet at the back of the yard and, next to the toilet, a coalshed. We had a fairly big yard with a mesh fence on all four sides. The only door into the house faced eastwards and led into our kitchen. Inside, from the door looking at the centre of the kitchen, stood an enamel table flanked by four chairs. To the left of the door there was a metal and glass cupboard whose powder-blue colour matched that of the tables and chairs. On the cupboard sat a Blaupunkt radio set that everyone called a wireless. From the main door, beyond the kitchen table, stood our trusted Defy coal stove – not quite the Welcome Dover made popular by Zulu folk singer Mbongeni Ngema, but a robust stove nonetheless. To the immediate right of the kitchen door was another door, leading to my mother's bedroom. Inside her bedroom was a double bed, always covered in thick and elaborately designed bedspreads, a wardrobe made of dark wood and a kist in which she kept her jewellery and best linen, to be brought out only for guests and on days such as Christmas. Echoes of Walter Benjamin's recollections of his Berlin childhood come to mind when I think about my mother's brooches, necklaces, special linen and china.

I can't say I liked my mother's bedroom. It was here, after all, that I had what I think was my first conscious brush with death one wintry Sunday. We had returned from church and I was napping on her bed while she was outside in the coalshed picking up coal and firewood for the evening's fire. One of the candles used to illuminate the room fell on the light-brown chequered *tapyt* with dark brown squares. The *tapyt* caught fire, which spread on to the curtains, and before my Mom knew it, the whole room was ablaze, with me, still only a toddler, caught in the middle of the conflagration. Mother and neighbours came into the room just in time to save me – but not before I had incurred second-degree burns to my right elbow and minor burns to my scalp. The burns left me with scars that earned me the nickname Kentucky Fried Chicken Wing at primary school. I was taken to Natalspruit,

Township in Sight

the hospital about a kilometre to the south-west of us. But I was too young to remember many of the details, except the terror of that room. Although the room was repainted shortly after the incident, I could, in my mind, still see smoke patches on the roof for years afterwards. It was a while before I could sleep in that room by myself or venture into it in the dark. Today, just thinking about the incident, I can still smell the smoke and see the burnt *tapyt*.

My favourite room in the house was the one farthest away from the door leading into the house. This was our dining room cum lounge. The room was painted a light cream colour, giving it an airy sunnyness. The room had a glass door partitioning it from the kitchen, and inside was a sideboard made of solid imbuia wood that preserved Mother's best china and the forks and knives that came out only on special days. There was also a brown wooden bookshelf heaving with books that belonged to Solly, a relative studying to be a medical technician, and my Uncle Abel. My favourites were the atlases and English grammar books, which I claimed as my own. The dining room was not quite the museum of Orhan Pamuk's grandmother but still it was a timepiece to be used only by guests and on special occasions. All the same, I would steal into the room whenever I could, pull out an atlas or grammar book from the bookshelf and climb on to a red sleeper couch – for years my favourite piece of furniture in the house – and read to my heart's content. Occasionally, I would fall asleep on the couch, clutching whatever book I had. It was a warm house.

It was also a working-class home. When Katlehong was built in 1949, families with the means to build their own houses were allowed to do so under an assisted home-ownership scheme. In this way middle-class sections emerged such as Maphanga, Credi, Moshoeshoe and Monaheng. Families, such as ours, which did not have the means to build their own homes were treated as lodgers and charged economic rentals on municipal property. They were placed in sections such as Makula, Mopedi, Phake, Twala, Hlahatsi and Nhlapo, where I grew up. The difference in housing types made visible the class differences within Katlehong. In fact, a Katlehong resident named Joe Mashao told Philip Bonner and Noor Nieftagodien: 'It was possible to recognise poor people more clearly. Even today, you can recognise differences between the children of people from Nhlapo to those from Monaheng.'

The ethnic mix of Katlehong's original northern sections was remarkable enough by the first decade of apartheid rule for a Dutch sociologist who studied Katlehong in the 1950s to comment on it. The sociologist must have known this was down to sheer luck. The sections were built in 1949, barely a year after the Nationalists won power with promises to put the kaffir in his place and only three years before Hendrik Verwoerd – who would go on to become Prime Minister from 1958 to 1966 – stamped his authority on so-called native administration in South Africa. It was Verwoerd who, in addition to pushing for the creation of homelands, instructed apartheid town planners and white administrators of black areas to see to it that every township was segregated along tribal lines. I have sometimes wondered what the local government official who allocated my Granny and Mother their houses would have done with my 'mixed' family – a family that was as Zulu (my

Township in Sight

mother's preferred language) as it was Sotho (Grandmother's first language).

As with the Hutus and Tutsis of Rwanda, there is no such thing as a Zutho (Zulu-Sotho) in southern Africa. Your ethnicity is determined by your father's identity. But there were no men in my family. So, even though my maternal grandfather Mabote was a Mosotho, my mother identified herself as Zulu but spoke Sotho and a few other languages, including Afrikaans. Anyway, our luck at being among the first of Katlehong's inhabitants meant that I grew up with a cacophony of languages, more Babelic archipelago than the ethnic islands desired and imagined by apartheid planners. The neighbours whose front door faced ours were the Pedi-speaking Brother Lucas and his lovely young wife Diana. The house behind ours, the one to which ours was attached, was a Sotho household headed by four formidable sisters, one of whom was the mother of one of my childhood friends, Mubi (Sotho for 'ugly'). Across the street from us lived Mrs Nkosi, a Swazi, and the house attached to hers belonged to Mrs Chancele, a Xhosa woman whose real name I never learnt. Chancele was a name given to her by the neighbourhood because she used to organise pilgrimages to Chancele, a village in the Eastern Cape where there resided a prophetess. One of my mother's best friends, Mrs Buthelezi, was a Zulu and her house was opposite the Roman Catholic church. Attached to Mrs Buthelezi's house was the Chirwas' house. Mr Chirwa was a Malawian migrant famous in our street for three things: his stern and hyper-religious wife, immaculate garden (the only one in our street that boasted the type of grass adults said was

Native Nostalgia

used at Wimbledon – not the more common Kikuyu grass), and mangled Zulu. The last attribute made Mr Chirwa a source of private jokes in our street. Once, following the massive 1982 snow storm that brought Johannesburg and its surrounds to a standstill, I went to Mr Chirwa's house on some errand for my mother. Our business concluded, Mr Chirwa led me to his gate and, looking at the sky, said: 'Nibona ngathi lizakikirika futhi [It looks like it's going to snow again].' Except, there is no such word as *kikirika* in Zulu. The word he was looking for was *khithika* (from the infinitive *ukukhithika*, to snow). It was not long after that episode that Mr Chirwa became, especially to my Aunt Z, who loved to rib people, Mr Kikirika. There were other characters in our street, such as the Zulu man whose house faced Mrs Buthelezi's who so loved women with big behinds that he called them *izipakupaku* (Zulu for 'drums'). He became Mr Sipakupaku – Mr Drum.

Like most streets in Katlehong at the time, ours was not tarred. Nonetheless, the Roman Street was still a major terrain of social encounters and a place of pleasure and anxiety. The Sotho sisters who lived behind us ran a shebeen, a place of pleasure, while to the east of the Roman Catholic church, at the bottom of our block, was an open plot of land which was a place of anxiety, a notorious mugging spot, especially on Friday nights when labourers would be returning home with their pay packets for the week, fortnight or month. Our street was also a terrain of encounters between neighbours and strangers, mostly friendly but sometimes violent, even deadly. The first dead body I ever saw belonged to a man who had been drinking at the shebeen next door, had got into a

Township in Sight

fight with someone (never identified) and been stabbed in the chest. The man staggered out of the shebeen and, too drunk to walk anywhere, collapsed across the street from our house. By the time an ambulance came for him, a neighbour had already covered his cold body with a blanket. I could not have been older than 10 then.

To think nostalgically about the streets on which I grew up is to think longingly of a lost world, a world in which dead bodies were treated with more respect than seems to be the case at present. It is to think also of the famous exchange described so movingly by Albie Sachs, in his essay 'Preparing Ourselves for Freedom', between artist Dumile Feni and a critic. The critic, watching a policeman harass a group of men to demand that they produce their passes, asks Feni a question that goes something like this: 'Why don't you depict that in your art?' At that very moment, a funeral cortège drives past and the harassed men turn towards the convoy, take off their hats and kneel down. Feni, looking at the men, turns to the critic: 'Now that is what I want to paint.' Or words to that effect. The story might actually be apocryphal, given the uncanny way it echoes a story recounted by Walter Benjamin and Asja Lacis about a priest being hounded out of town for a social infraction. As the crowd marches through town with the priest in front, a funeral cortège (or was it a wedding?) goes by at that very moment. Everyone stops and the priest is asked to bless the passersby. He does. The passersby move on. The hounding of the priest resumes. In both stories there is a quiet dignity and respect for the dead in the midst of daily humiliations that resonates. Reading about the men's gesture in Sachs's story reminds me that this is what we used to do. Sadly, we no longer kneel for the dead.

However, there was more to the sidewalk ballet than the occasional tragedy. There were the regular waves of workers who would flow up and down our street – a major pedestrian thoroughfare connecting the interior of Nhlapo and other sections to the Katlehong railway station and the taxi rank on the northern edge of the township. Katlehong was a township of people constantly on the move. We were among a handful of families on the street that used the coalsheds at the back of our properties for their original purpose. Most families simply rented theirs out to migrant workers and homeless families. One of these coalshed tenants in our street was a Xhosa man from the Eastern Cape who seemed to own only the clothes on his back and would wash them every day after work, earning himself the nickname Mr Was-ayilinde, Mr Wash-and-wait, used behind his back of course. There were other participants in this sidewalk ballet. The most memorable of these were itenarant Ndebele traders, who sold brooms and mielies. It was said that their muti was so potent no one dared insult or mug them. They would tell anyone stupid enough to try: 'Ulibambe lingashoni' (Don't let the sun set). When it did, it would go down with you. Other inhabitants of our street included the drunkards who would stagger up and down the street all weekend long, the families going to Germiston for their shopping, the families in their Sunday best going to church and the hipsters, pantsulas and punks strutting their fashions up and down the street. Occasionally, drum majorettes would appear from nowhere, march down

Township in Sight

the street and disappear just as quickly.

Then there was always Mrs Nkosi, our Swazi neighbour. No one in our street could swear like her. The best way to imagine her effect is to picture the quintessential scene in a western where a town square goes dead in seconds as windows are closed and shutters pulled while the bad guy and his posse, spoiling for a fight, slowly ride into town, towards the main square where the hero-sheriff is already waiting outside a saloon, itchy hands by his sides, guns at the ready. Fortunately for our parents, Mrs Nkosi always announced her arrival in the metaphorical public square with a piercing 'Heyi!' as she strode to the edge of her fence, tucking the sides of her dress into her underwear as she did so. At her second 'Heyi!' our parents would already be outside, desperately urging us to run indoors before Mrs Nkosi let fly. They would drag us inside by the scruff of our necks and slam the doors shut behind us, to protect us from being corrupted by the bile coming out of Mrs Nkosi's mouth. I have never seen anyone clear a street the way Mrs Nkosi could with her swear words. Sometimes the children would drag their feet as mothers scrambled to close their ears, just so that they could hear how many new permutations of *msunu* (cunt), *mthondo* (dick), and *nuka* (smelly) Mrs Nkosi would conjure up this time. But any kid who dragged his feet too long risked a smack from his parents. It was never entirely clear what occasioned Mrs Nkosi's outbursts.

The neighbourhood kids were of course among the most active participants of the sidewalk ballet. We were among the first to pour on to the streets in the morning as we walked in

Native Nostalgia

different directions to school – the Zulu speakers to Zulu-medium schools, Sotho speakers to Sotho-medium schools and so on. Sometimes kids from the same household would go to different language schools, depending on their last names and on where their parents had bothered to register them. I went to Zulu-medium schools for lower and higher primary school (Monde and Izibuko) and to Ponego, a dual Zulu–Sotho-medium school, for the first two years of high school.

Historians have remarked on the tragic irony that at the same time that the apartheid state was systematically gutting quality black education – by destroying mission schools, introducing Bantu education – it was also presiding over an explosion in the number of black children enrolled in government schools. The increase in student numbers came at the same time that the state was losing good teachers and classes were getting overcrowded, with learners sharing desks meant for only a few. My first two years of school were spent not at Monde Primary, where I was enrolled, but platooning at two churches, including the neighbourhood Baptist church. Platooning was a system whereby classes were divided into groups. Group A would attend classes from 8 am to noon one week and afternoon classes (noon to 4 pm) the next, with groups alternating by the week.

I hated afternoon platoons because they left me with only two hours of play before I had to take my evening bath at 7 pm. For me, as I am sure for many of my friends, after-school play was the most important part of our street life. Here we played soccer, marbles, spinning tops, a cricket-like game called *bhathi*, a card game called boom, *umgusha* (high jump), kites,

Township in Sight

wire cars and, of course, black *mampatile* (hide-and-seek). But these were not just street games. They heralded in their own way the change in seasons. You could tell what season it was by watching which games children played. Local merchants would know what toys to stock by observing the sequence of games. This was not, however, a simple case of supply and demand but an illustration of a cosmology in which each segment played its part without having to be told what to do. There was, of course, a simple logic to this. Black *mampatile* was a winter game because the sun set early in winter, making it easy to find hiding spots in the dark where boys and girls could make out. There might also be a far more profound cosmology in the games children played. As Giorgio Agamben points out, children's games reveal a fusion between the world of play and that of the sacred.

In this fusion of play and the sacred, licence was granted, liberties taken and children got away with a lot. Game time was the only instance when children could get away with taking the mickey out of adults. And none could do this better than Thami, Mrs Chancele's son. A useless team player, Thami was nonetheless the most skilled ball-handler in the street. He could do things with a soccer ball that many of us could only marvel at. Except for weekends, we played most of our drop-four soccer games (games with no duration; the first team to score four goals won the match) on the street and in the afternoons, that is, at the same time that adults were streaming back from work. Thami had a particular skill whereby, with his back to the ball, he could use one foot to hit the ball against the other foot, flicking it up in the air and away from him as he did so. Of course he would time this trick just as a group of adults were walking towards him. He would wait until they were close enough before unleashing his missile, usually hitting one of them bang in the face. Because he performed the trick with his back to his victims, he would play dumb, looking first to his feet as if to say 'Where is my ball?', then would turn around and, feigning surprise that the ball had hit someone, apologise profusely to the victim. Sometimes his victims, with a round patch of dust on their faces, would chase Thami into his yard, calling him and his mother names as they did so.

But parents also had their own games. One was the Chinese numbers game, fahfee. Pretty much every household had a playing purse: a roundish leather bag with a zip on top. Numbers could be got from anywhere. Any dream, any incident (such as an irate adult chasing a laughing boy into a yard) could be translated into a fahfee number. The draw was every afternoon and the Chinese owner of the fahfee game would drive into our neighbourhood in an armoured car to meet with his African runners, who would have collected the players' purses earlier in the day, and reveal the day's lucky number. Sometimes, adults would mine children's dreams for numbers, scrutinising every aspect of a dream for possible number combinations. 'Sonny, now just try and recall. Where in the dream was your late grandmother when the dove shat on her? What was she wearing?' I can hear an adult interrogating a child for a winning number. If their selection won, the lucky child would be treated to sweets.

However, our street was not simply an everyday site of play, social encounters, and individual and group fashioning. It was also part of a world in flux. Katlehong, declared a city in the 1980s, might be a small place but it has been subject in some ways to the same local, national and international currents that have shaped Johannesburg, the elusive metropolis that is also South Africa's commercial capital, 30 kilometres to the west of us. In other words, Katlehong is not a zone of lack on the margins of the global political economy. It is part of this economy in ways that extend beyond the political. As Doreen Massey says, 'The global is in the local in the very process of the formation of the local.'

So far, I have sketched a background that identifies Katlehong on the map and illustrates, in an idiosyncratic fashion, Katlehong's place in the multiple elsewheres to which every place in this world is connected. The idea of multiple elsewheres is borrowed from Gillian Hart, who explains it thus: 'The concept of multiple trajectories and the method of relational comparison are grounded in an understanding of place not as a bounded unit, but as always formed through relations and connections with dynamics at play in other places, and in wider regional, national, and transnational arenas.' I have also shown in glib fashion how the economic sanctions imposed on apartheid South Africa played themselves out before the eyes of a young boy in the area when our Barclays Bank became First National Bank. I have shown how blind luck saw my family escape Verwoerd's injunction that Zulus be housed among Zulus, and what the legacy of his educational policies looked like to a 6-year-old going to an urban government school for the first time in his life.

Native Nostalgia

To speak of Katlehong's place in the world is to speak, in a broad sense, of South Africa's black urban history. This is a history that goes back much farther than the advent of apartheid in 1948. It goes back to the mineral revolution of the nineteenth century that followed the discovery of diamonds in Kimberley and gold on the Witwatersrand. This revolution, together with the labour regime it enacted and the land ownership patterns it inspired, spurred the waves of black urbanisation that saw Germiston, our 'white parent city', boast one of the largest black urban communities on the Reef by 1912. Such waves were given further momentum by the Second World War, which drew more Africans into the industrial economy. This connection to multiple elsewheres has not been severed, even if it might be different today from what it was fifty or a hundred years ago.

This book is not an ethnography of Katlehong, a systematic study of its culture, even though there is some of that. Nor is it a conventional retelling of Katlehong's history, with events flowing neatly into a chronological whole. There is no recounting of dates like the beads of a rosary. The book is neither a memoir nor indeed even a cultural biography of Katlehong. But it contains elements of both. This book is best understood as a gathering of fragments of memory, souvenirs of the imagination. I have collected these fragments into a fractured whole through which I hope to look back at a life, a childhood, spent under apartheid. But this should not be taken to mean that what follows is a lament. There is nothing mournful about these pages. There was nothing mournful about my township childhood, despite standard portrayals

Township in Sight

of township life that sometimes paint it as miserable. As Italo Calvino reminds us in his novel *Invisible Cities*, one should never confuse the description of a thing with the thing itself. That is to say, one should never take the standard description of townships as poor to mean that township life was poor.

But what, then, of the problems of the area? Problems there are, aplenty. As I write this, I can look out of the main window in our lounge to see young men going in and out of the local drug dealer's house. I can walk up and down the street to see the many backyard shacks that have sprung up in my neighbourhood as unemployed homeowners use their properties to make ends meet and desperate homeless people pay whatever rent is demanded of them. I can also walk around the neighbourhood to see government schools, including some I went to as a young man, that have mastered the art of churning out educated illiterates: students who spend their entire careers being taught in English and yet would not know a verb even if it cornered them behind a shack and offered them drugs at a discount. Then there are the invisible problems: people my age and younger rotting away in poorly lit bedrooms as HIV/AIDS claims their lives inch by inch, day by day. We know they are there because we don't see them on the streets, which is where the neighbourhood meets. But we also know they are there because people gossip, especially about the misfortunes of others.

These are by no means the only problems that exist in Katlehong. I only have to walk around our yard in the morning to see the fresh, dark droppings of rats, the township's most prolific residents. In the rats, which seem to have overrun every township, I sometimes feel my nostalgia turn to disgust. But it was not always so.

3

Strangers from Underground

In your case, the worst thing in the world happens to be rats.
– George Orwell, *Nineteen Eighty-four*

In December 2007 a friend and I reported on the ANC's conference in Polokwane as correspondents for *The Weekender*, *Business Day*'s weekend edition. I was supposed to arrange accommodation for us but left it so late that, by the time I did, the only place available was a truck stop on the southern edge of Polokwane. The place was overrun with cockroaches. The roaches were in every crevice: in the shower, on the bed, under the bed, in the cupboards, on the window sills. They were everywhere. You could not take two steps without stepping on one. It almost felt as if, in coming to the ANC conference, we had found ourselves bang in the middle of a roaches' convention. I cannot eat in a place where I see a roach and will not stay in a place with roaches. But I was not going to miss the ANC conference, what with Jacob Zuma about to become president and Thabo Mbeki sent packing. No cockroach was going to make me miss the showdown.

So I went out and bought insect-repellent sprays, having extracted a promise from the woman running the motel that

Native Nostalgia

she would reimburse me. (She never did.) The conference ran for five days. Each day, I would wake up early, spray the room silly with insect-repellent, go to the conference to watch the ANC tear itself apart, return to the room in the evening to kill some more roaches, sleep, wake up the next day to spray once again and then go watch the ANC destroy itself. It was an odd ritual. Somehow it seemed to fit with the times, when erstwhile comrades were speaking of each other as political vermin, something to be exterminated. It was obvious that, for some people in the ANC, there was more at stake than simple questions of who was to get what, where and when. It was war: exterminate or be exterminated. I could relate to this. After all, I was involved in a daily campaign of extermination against the vermin in my room. It was a campaign to the death and its roots lay deep within me. I have a pathological hatred of roaches, which I inherited from my mother. However, my hatred of roaches is nothing compared with my loathing and fear of rats. For me, rats are indeed the worst thing in the world.

The rat occupies a special place in South African struggle mythology. *Igundwane*, Nguni for rat, is what you call a scab; *amagundwane* is what you call scab labourers. In struggle-speak, to be a rat is to be a traitor, vermin. It is not uncommon to hear striking workers shout: 'Bulalani amagundwane! Kill the scabs.' It is also not uncommon to hear of people being hacked to death, thrown off trains, doused with petrol and set alight – all for being scabs and crossing the picket line. To be a rat, then, is to be forever marked for gruesome death.

I am not a scab and do not think that I am marked for

death. But there may be hacks who see my question of what it means to be nostalgic for a life lived under apartheid as a sign of treachery. To these people, my attempt to upset the neat master narrative of the struggle in which blacks suffered and struggled the same, might constitute behaviour no different from that of a rat. If these readers were indeed to think that way about this book, it would be, for a township boy like me, an ironic case of a hunter becoming the hunted.

In a book on the rodents of southern Africa published in 1981, Gerrit de Graaff listed the following as being among the predators of the yellow-footed squirrel: hawks, owls, genets, wild cats, pythons and 'Black children using dogs and sticks'. We did not have squirrels in Katlehong when I was growing up, but the first time I read De Graaff's book, I recalled an encounter in the early 1980s between my cousin S and a rodent. Cousin S was on his way to the local shops when, as he was cutting a double lap behind a neighbour's coalshed, he came face to face with a rat, a white rat. He instinctively picked up a rock while the rat stared him down, threw it and knocked the rat dead. Satisfied with a hit job well done, S went on his way, leaving the dead rat lying behind. He had not gone far when he heard a scream. It turned out that the rat was a neighbour's pet that had escaped from its cage. This explained why the thing had stared at S while he picked up his rock, instead of scampering off as the rats we were used to would have done.

Unfortunately for S, a neighbour saw him kill the pet and it wasn't long before the pet owner confronted my mother, demanding compensation for her loss and punishment for my cousin. To keep the peace in the neighbourhood, Mother

Native Nostalgia

accepted the neighbour's demands. S and I were about to go on a trip for a karate tournament but Mother decided that, as punishment, S would not go. S was devastated. We had been waiting for the trip for a year. But we were also incredulous. Who in his right mind kept rats as pets in Katlehong? In fact, who on earth kept rats as pets? We could not believe it. As De Graaff so expertly put it, we black children preyed on rodents. We would go on hunting trips against rodents, using fire to smoke them out of their holes and stones to finish them off.

There were two kinds of rats when I was growing up: a striped rat we called *imbiba* and a big rodent we called *iroto*. The former you could eat; the latter you would not touch even if your life depended on it. For some reason, *imbiba* was considered more hygienic than the slightly bigger *roto*. It was also believed that eating *imbiba* could help bed-wetters get over their problem. But I could never understand why hunting *imbiba* was such a big deal. Hunting the bloody things was a lot of work for very little reward. *Imbibas* are such small rodents that you have to kill hundreds in one hunt and skewer them in a straightened hanger to have enough to eat. But hunt them we did. It was part of the fun of growing up in a township.

Looking back on my childhood, I can't help thinking that part of what made rat-hunting such fun was that rats were not a common sight in our neighbourhood. They were there but they were not as ubiquitous as they seem to be today. Nowadays, the rat problem has become so big in South African townships that tabloids have been feasting on the hysteria generated by the rodents. Municipalities have had to introduce owls to deal with the problem. In Katlehong, the municipal council has even hosted a 'rat summit' – such is the scale of the epidemic. For someone like me, with a pathological aversion to rats of any kind, the apparent profusion of rats has induced a new sense in me: dread. It is as if the whole township has become Orwell's Room 101, where we each meet our worst nightmares. There is nothing like the sight of a big grey rat, long rubbery tail in tow, to fill my entire body with loathing.

According to RatZooMan, a European Union-funded research project intended to examine the prevalence of plague-bearing rats in southern Africa, 'South Africa is a plague-endemic country and needs to have ongoing surveillance in place.' The plague, which wiped out a quarter of Europe's population in the Middle Ages, swept through South Africa during the Anglo-Boer War in 1899–1902, killing thousands of people. Rodents are vectors of diseases such as leptospirosis, toxoplasmosis, rabies, trichinosis, murine typhus, relapsing fever, plague, helminthes and salmonellosis, to mention a few. They are nasty little creatures and we are right to dread them.

Who can't but feel a sense of revulsion when tabloids keep telling us that our rats have got so big that cats, or at least the handful one finds in Katlehong, dare not approach them. Every so often, one local rag in particular will run stories showing pictures of corpses that have allegedly been gnawed at by massive rats, called *amagalpentsi* in some townships, in unkempt government mortuaries. There are also reports of babies who have been killed in their sleep by rats. As one scientific paper put it: 'Recent newspaper articles have dramatized the apparent increase in ... rodent populations, often exaggerating their physical size and spreading panic.'

Native Nostalgia

The paper said that residents of Durban's informal settlements viewed rodents as 'primary competitors for scarce resources. There are many tales of rats performing amazing and brazen thefts of food, such as opening lids on a food source.' It actually does not matter whether what the newspapers and people say about rats is true. It is enough simply that there are sufficient numbers of these four-legged creatures to induce panic in many people. Perhaps in the rat, democratic South Africa may have found a more fearsome and enduring symbol than the criminal.

Although I do not know if this is a question of life imitating art, I do find it telling that in its broad outlines Winston's nightmare in Orwell's *Nineteen Eighty-four* echoes some of the standard tabloid tales told about rats in South Africa. Listen to the torturer O'Brien torment Winston: 'The rat ... although a rodent, is carnivorous. You are aware of that. You will have heard of the things that happen in the poor quarters of this town. In some streets a woman dare not leave her baby alone, even for five minutes. The rats are certain to attack it. Within quite a small time they will strip it to the bones. They also attack sick or dying people. They show astonishing intelligence in knowing when a human being is helpless.'

In the rat, it seems to me, all the fears, anxieties, hysteria and uncertainty come together that make living in South Africa today such a nerve-racking experience. I once wrote a column asking where all these big rats came from. Many people responded with obvious answers about human population increases, the spread of informal settlements, poor hygiene in many of these places and shoddy service delivery by the government. However, one colleague suggested that the big rats we see in South Africa's big cities, especially the former mining areas around Johannesburg, might actually come from abandoned and flooded former mines. According to this man, rats are to South African mines what canaries were to European mines. He said it was all well and good when the mines, which are some of the deepest in the world, were still operational. Then the rats underground could get fed through the constant human traffic going up and down the shafts. But with the closure of many mines and their flooding due to lack of maintenance and to prevent illegal mining, the rats had nowhere to go but up. If this is indeed the case, the denizens of South Africa's economic foundations, the mines, may be coming to the surface to claim some of what belongs to them. The rat, then, may be the symbol par excellence of Gauteng's duality as a place of the ground and the underground.

This duality is brought out by Achille Mbembe and Sarah Nuttall in their book *Johannesburg: The Elusive Metropolis*. They point out that the city would not have existed without mining. In other words, the city owes its existence to the subterranean. They write: 'It is at these deeper levels and in the way the world below interacted with the surface and the edges that the origins of the city as a metropolis are to be located. Beneath the central business district and the environs of Johannesburg lie thousands of boreholes and drilling footages of varying depths …' To be sure, Mbembe and Nuttall are writing about Johannesburg, but their observations hold true for the conurbation that contains Katlehong. Cities such as Germiston, Boksburg and Benoni also owed their existence to the same processes that led to the founding of Johannesburg. Townships such as Katlehong, Vosloorus and Daveyton grew out of the same economic and cultural drives that made Gauteng, the place of gold, the commercial and cultural capital of South Africa. Again, as Mbembe and Nuttall point out, for far too long 'the township' has been treated as a marginal 'site of social struggles or of contestation over the allocation of public goods'. This treatment has tended to ignore the ways in which townships are 'both of the city and not of the city'.

In the rodents that roam the townships today, one is confronted with both the past of urban South Africa with its underground origins and the fragility of the new order. There is seemingly not much we can do to control the rat epidemic. Wherever humans are, rats will always find a niche for themselves. In the rat problem, we are also shown the limits of state power. There is only so much the government can do – and getting rid of rats is not one of those competencies.

One saw this failure in the hamfisted way the municipality that controls Katlehong went about its business of pest control when residents started complaining about the rats. It introduced owls. A resident of Thokoza, the small township to the west of Katlehong, told a focus group that the rats were so big, not even owls knew how to tackle them. 'What owl in its right mind would attack a rat that can stand on two legs?' The council was aware of the fact that owls occupy a negative place in township cosmologies. They are associated with witchcraft. Some people believe that seeing an owl during the day means the same thing as seeing a black cat in broad daylight: death for you or someone close to you. The council knew this. After all, the majority of the people running the council today come from townships. It does not matter that these views are quaint, nonsensical or downright silly. However, the council believed that residents would change their views about owls overnight – all because the council told them to. Well, they were wrong. People started killing the owls with as much enthusiasm as the hated rats – and this they did with no intention of spiting the council. In fact, some of them did not even know that the owls had been brought in by the council to feed on the rats.

One relative, a good marksman, took to shooting owls as they perched on electricity poles. He had no time for the righteous nonsense being peddled by the municipality. The rats might have been a nuisance but at least, for him, they were not the omen that the owls were. It took a while to persuade him that seeing an owl during the day did not mean certain death. But many residents still see owls as a greater evil than rats, even though there are more of the latter. It also seems not to matter that rats are, in the greater scheme of things, certainly more dangerous than owls ever could be. In a sense, one must feel sorry for the municipality. How can it possibly be expected to factor witchcraft into its planning strategy?

In talking about the clash between instrumentalist reason as exemplified by the government and township cosmologies that cannot be subjected easily to such reason, I am also trying to extend Mbembe and Nuttall's argument about the connection between the visible and the invisible in the making of South Africa's commercial capital. They write: 'In fact, the entire history of Johannesburg's built structures testifies not only to its inscription into the canons of modern Western urban aesthetics, but also to the originary tension virtually built into its morphology and geological structure between the life below the surface, what is above, and the edges.' Put another way, the coming of the rats might be my nightmare, my Room 101, come true. But it is in a larger sense Gauteng and its political economy opening up to the world. The rats might be a bad dream come true for me. But they are in effect among some of greater Johannesburg's original inhabitants.

Although, according to De Graaff, there are '73 rodent species known to occur in southern Africa', I think it would be fair to say that in townships such as Katlehong, there are two rodent species known to occur there: big rats and very big rats. That, at any rate, is what many township residents seem to think. I was persuaded of this when I heard a 4-year-old grandnephew make what has now become a standard township rat joke: 'The rats are so big they look like cats.' The boy's comment was made all the more interesting by the fact that, as the township pet-owning business goes, there are very few cats around. In fact, there is a greater chance that the boy has yet to see a real cat and only knows about them from talk or TV. No matter, it is probably just as good that possibly every township kid knows what rats look like. Properly channelled, this could be their first lesson in the urban history of southern Africa.

As Mbembe and Nuttall say, 'In many senses, there is no metropolis without a necropolis. Just as the metropolis is closely linked to monuments, artifacts, technological novelty, an architecture of light and advertising, the phantasmagoria of selling, and a cornucopia of commodities, so it is produced by what lies below the surface.' This makes me wonder, though, if the dread I feel at the sight of a big township rat is not perhaps an aversion to a side of South African history that has always been there but is often talked about only in terms of political economy. My sense of dread is real enough. But it comes only when I see the rats, not when I think in abstract terms of the origins of South Africa's economy. That is why, I think, it is so important to start writing histories of urban South Africa that more consciously foreground the senses.

To do that would be one way of confronting the legacy of apartheid. As Mbembe and Nuttall write, 'The work of apartheid was to make sure that these lower depths of the city, without which its modernity was unreadable, were made to appear as strangers to the city, apart from the city.' The challenge perhaps is to see the rats that today populate urban South Africa in ever-increasing numbers as an integral part of the city. We should not see them as strangers that have suddenly appeared from we don't know where.

Here, we might even extend this point to confront the way in which we tend to talk about the bodies that populate the two hundred or so informal settlements around greater Johannesburg and the East Rand. As more and more mines throw their workers above the surface and into a sea of redundancy and superfluity, many of these former mineworkers have flocked to the informal settlements. With nothing but the certainty of a bare life to return to in their rural areas, former miners have opted to eke out an existence on the margins of the cities they helped build. They have chosen to survive in the informal settlements which are home to many of the rats that have seized the popular imagination and sparked such fear and hysteria. Not quite sure what to make of people who have appeared on the surface as if from nowhere, many of us are asking: 'Who are these strangers in our midst? Where do they come from?' The miners can of course answer back but they do not seem interested in justifying their existence.

It seems to me now that, by seeing the rat epidemic purely as a public health issue, one would be blinding oneself to one of the greatest revenges of history possible. Greater Johannesburg, not to mention Katlehong and its environs, may be among the most segregated cities in the world. But, as we know from the European plague in the Middle Ages, the Black Death did not care for social distinction. It was as equally brutal with the nobility as it was with the common people. It may also be that in the rat, which is just as prevalent in places of privilege as it is in poor areas, South Africa also faces one of the greatest social and epidemic levellers we have ever seen; something akin, in fact, to HIV/AIDS. Interestingly, many of the diseases borne by rats are not necessarily fatal to humans – save for individuals with compromised immune systems because of conditions such as HIV/AIDS. This may be just one of the many ways in which South Africans are forced to confront – despite the panic, hysteria and exaggerations inspired by everything from crime and corruption to rodents – the many problems we share in common. For my part, I am not interested simply in the racialised social distinctions that traditionally define South Africa. I am also keen at examining social distinction as a key historical feature of black life. Black South Africans may experience the rat epidemic the same way. But that does not mean they are the same.

4
Class Warfare

In a real sense, I do not have to dig too deeply into the memories of my childhood to realise that, thanks to my primary school teachers, I knew who my social betters were long before I knew what they were. That is to say, I knew there were schoolmates who were a class above me long before I understood there was such a thing as social distinction. My schoolfellows and I at Monde Primary wore the same uniform: white shirts, red jerseys and black shorts. But underneath all that lurked social distinctions that were prevented from displaying themselves largely by a state that did not care to distinguish between a black doctor and a black domestic. So it was that a teacher's daughter found herself at the same school as the shoeless son of a gardener. But the differences did show themselves (not just in winter when you could tell by looking at who wore shoes and who did not), and our modestly educated teachers proved themselves the most ardent defenders of such class distinctions. Thus it was that in a school whose playground was full of boys with names such as Abednego, Bethuel and

Zebulon, and girls called Granny, Salamina and Tryphina, those so named tended to find themselves in classrooms lettered C and downwards. On the other hand, the Nompumelelos and Khayas took rooms A and B, officially the top classes in a grade. Hardly anyone remarked on the fact that the kids with the African names, who happened to be the spawn of priests, doctors, nurses, teachers and government clerks, were literally in a class of their own, regardless of academic ability. They were members of our high society. *Ama-high soss*, we called them, top *shayelas*, children of *amarespectables*, *izihlonishwa*. That was enough. Their names marked them out. But, then again, the black elite did seem to aspire to a racial authenticity which they felt detached from by virtue of their social standing.

It is not that those of us running around the school playground with labels such as Abednego and Zebulon did not have African names. We did. But those were *amagam' asekhaya* (home names), and school was a serious matter, not a place for uncouth home names. Without the confidence that seemed to come easily to the black elite, our working-class parents took seriously the business of Christian names for *amagam' esikole* (school names). Later on, some parents would go easy on the Bible as a source of forenames, opting for gems like Surprise. I must admit, though, that I could not understand the whole commerce of naming in my neighbourhood. People who would kill you in a second for naming a dog after them, would not think twice of calling their child Matlakala (Rubbish), Makaka (Shit) or Mubi (Ugly). And don't think their children shied away from using these names. They bore them with pride, some even shortening them to hipper versions: Matlaks for

Class Warfare

Matlakala, MaCakes for Makaka and Mubzin for Mubi. As for our social betters, they went by their African names and nothing else. Freedom might have seemed a long way off in the early 1980s but, like a conqueror drunk with anticipation of a victory written in the stars, the cocky black elite had, with help from our teachers, sent its young advance guard to our school playground to let us know who was who in the zoo.

At school the rigid enforcers of class distinctions were the staff. Mrs M, the tall, elegant but stern headmistress to whom I was related on my father's side, would not pass on a chance to remind us, barely in our teens, that she was well educated. This was more than could be said for our parents, and we daren't forget it. Mrs M was a keen chorister who seemed more interested in turning every girl into a mellifluous soprano and every boy into an ace tenor than in producing A students. She would force us to drink castor oil and suck on Sen-Sen sweets to 'improve' our voices. She would sometimes come to assembly, where we sang the virtues of Jesus Christ every morning, bearing in hand a cheese and tomato sandwich on white bread. Pity the barefoot urchin who looked at the sandwich while the headmistress waved it up and down like a baton as she conducted our singing. 'Yini! Awudlang' ekhaya? [What! Your family didn't feed you?]' she would say in a voice shrill in intent and contralto in pitch. If the scamp was lucky, he would be told to mind his manners next time. If the headmistress was feeling energetic, the poor thing would be hauled to the 'Principal's Office' – always referred to in English and pronounced in such a way you knew both words were capitalised – for a thrashing.

The Nompumelelos and Thembas were rarely at the receiving end of such attention. How could they be? Their parents were on first-name terms with the headmistress and her family, worshipped at the same church, had probably gone to the same schools and universities, and, I presume, regularly swapped LPs, from Beethoven to the latest in choral music from America. These were children who did not walk to school like the rest of us. They were driven to and fro in a sleek powder-blue bus called a Coaster. They were also children who did not have to hide should they, God forbid, come across the headmistress's car or any of our teachers in the streets on a weekend. They were the pride and joy of the school, future members of the local nobility. Meanwhile, the rest of us, usually dusty on weekends from playing street soccer, would know, the moment we saw the car or teacher, that we had booked ourselves a lashing come Monday morning. How dare we embarrass such a prestigious school like that, all dusty and looking like a *vuilpop*!

Monde prided itself on being the best school in Katlehong: the best in having, in Mrs M, one of the most highly educated principals in the township; the best in educating its young charges. But none of this seemed to please Mrs M more than the school's record in regularly winning choral music competitions. Monde was always guaranteed at least two trophies in the annual school competitions which began in the township and then moved to the school district and beyond as the school kept on singing its way to further accolades. In making Monde a choral powerhouse, Mrs M was doing no more than what came instinctively to someone of her background. She was in a way reminding us that South Africa's Christianised black elite was born singing. It was, after all, in mission stations that those who formed the modern black elite had found their voices. In these stations, learning to read and write went hand in hand with learning to sing the virtues of God. That is how choral music became a key part of the black elite's identity.

There is another reason why music was such an important part of the elite's identity. As Pierre Bourdieu says, 'nothing more clearly affirms one's "class", nothing more infallibly classifies, than taste in music'. This is because, says Bourdieu, 'Music is the most "spiritual" of the arts of the spirit and a love of music is a guarantee of "spirituality".' It certainly felt that way with our headmistress and her teachers. It was not just cleanliness that, for them, was close to godliness. Singing ability seemed to be closer to spirituality than whether we understood germ theory. And of course, being herself a product of colonial missionary beliefs in improvement, Mrs M believed that every student's voice could be improved.

It was not that our working-class parents were not partial to singing and good voices; they were. But their tastes tended to the more proletarian sounds of black urban South Africa. So we grew up listening to mbaqanga and isicathamiya, using the vinyls collected by my mother and her brothers, some of whom sang isicathamiya. In fact, the very first concert I ever attended was a Ladysmith Black Mambazo performance at the D.H. Williams Hall some time in the early 1980s. I remember seeing members of the famous a cappella group hours before the show started. They all had handkerchiefs covering their mouths. Long used to 'seeing' them through our wireless, it was exhilarating to see the faces behind the voices. They looked like my uncles, some of them. This was long before their reach extended beyond the then Radio Zulu and before their 'discovery' by Paul Simon. As David Coplan says, the black working class had its own musical culture, of which my family partook proudly. Mahlathini, the gruff-voiced leader of the Mahotella Queens, lived a street away from us. Jacob Mpharanyana Radebe, lead singer of a group called the Cannibals and considered by some to have been South Africa's finest soul singer of the 1970s, lived in my section.

But if, as Bourdieu says, 'taste classifies, and it classifies the classifier', my mother's taste in music marked her out as non-parochial in a weird way. She was also a big fan of Jim Reeves, the American country music singer who died in a plane crash in 1964. We had a whole stack of Reeves's vinyls when I was growing up. My mother was not alone in her liking of Reeves and his music. Apparently, Reeves had armies of supporters among the black working class in South Africa. He toured South Africa in 1963, recorded a number of Afrikaans songs and even starred in a local film entitled *Kimberley Jim*. I don't know if Mrs M, my primary school headmistress, was also partial to Reeves. I doubt it. I suspect Reeves would have been too low-class for her, too common. But it did not bother us one bit. There were millions of other working-class families like ours and we had a culture all our own. Needless to say, this was not an insular culture that failed to draw on influences from other classes and countries. The popularity in townships of Reeves and other types of music considered low-class, such

Class Warfare

as the American blues, proved this point.

There were other lessons that our school imprinted on our young minds. In fact, long before many of us had met a single white man, we already knew that one did not want to be dark-skinned. Long before we had direct experience of racism, we were taught that there were black people and there were black people. Nothing illustrates this point better than the following story. In my higher primary school years, I shared a class with two girls both named Maria. Mr Nhlapo, our mathematics teacher and one of the best teachers in the school, said he could not be bothered to explain which Maria he was calling each time he used the name. So Mr Nhlapo gave both girls new names. The two girls were quite dark in complexion. One came originally from Soweto and the other from a farming area not far from Katlehong called Tamboekisfontein. Mr Nhlapo decided he would call the girls Mantsho Soweto and Mantsho Tamboekies. (Mantsho is Sotho for 'darkie'.)

The colour of a person's skin did not have much to do with social distinction. After all, many of our social betters were just as dark-skinned as many of us. There were also working-class kids who were light-skinned. These often found themselves nicknamed 'Boesman guitar', a derogatory term usually reserved for South Africans of mixed descent. But knowing that there was such a thing as shadism (discrimination based on the shade of one's skin) and that anti-black racism did not need white agents to make itself felt was one of the best lessons I took away with me. It is from then that I learnt not to make easy assumptions about racial solidarities. The fact that someone looked like you phenotypically did not mean

Native Nostalgia

they agreed with you politically. Interestingly, many of our teachers at higher primary school had lived through the Black Power years and some of them had even taken part in the 1976 students' uprising. And yet here they were, calling their own students darkies.

Although dark-skinned, I was spared the indignity that came with Mr Nhlapo's nicknames by the fact that I was a diligent student. This did not mean he intervened when some of my classmates called me Kentucky Fried Chicken Wing because of the burn marks on my right elbow. Not that I needed his protection: I could look after myself and usually gave as good as I got. But there was something I could not escape: this was the fact that I came from a township and was therefore, in the eyes of some people who did not care much for townships, contaminated by whatever corrupting influences they assumed came from these places. According to them, townships were dens of iniquity and nothing good could possibly come out of them. In fact, student protests against Bantu education were believed by these people to be a disease and township kids were thought to be incurable carriers of the virus. Here is how I discovered this.

It is 1986, my first year of high school, and black schooling has come to a virtual standstill in Katlehong. Though Ponego Secondary, my school, is already a few years old at this point, it still has no premises of its own, leaving its students to squat at Samson Primary School. Samson's pupils are, in turn, shacking up somewhere else in the township. The lack of schooling means there will be no mid-year tests or final exams in November. For some of my classmates this is a minor

Class Warfare

inconvenience but for me a major tragedy. It means that, for the first time since I started school in 1979, I have no bargaining chip to use against my mother. I cannot use my exam results to ask for what I want. I cannot show her the envelope containing my results and say, while she is busy studying it, 'Mama, may I please have a pair of Dickies trousers? May I please have a pair of Kruger trousers? May I have a pair of All Star tackies?' I cannot ask for any of this. 'Hhayi suka wena! Get out of here. Why would I dress my son up in tsotsi attire,' she would ask rhetorically.

It was true. Tsotsis, township toughs, had cornered the Dickies, Kruger and All Star market. But what was a boy to do? For these also happened to be the hippest clothes out there. That is not to say *botsotsi* were the only people who wore this township 'uniform'. *Amapantsula* wore the same type of clothes, but for my mother and most adults there was no difference between *botsotsi* and *amapantsula*. They were like 6 and 9: the same thing, only flipped.

If I was feeling braver, I would ask Mother for Saxone shoes and Brentwood trousers. 'Uyaphambana kemanje [Now, you are going mad],' she would say. But I would always get an appropriate gift as a reward: a shirt, a tee, a pair of shoes or, better, new soccer cleats. However, for as long as I could remember, this was an exchange founded on a simple transaction: I would score in the top three in my class and Mother would acknowledge my achievement with a reward. There had not been a time in my eight years of schooling when this arrangement did not hold. Until 1986, that is. I had no results to show and could not, therefore, ask for new clothes.

Native Nostalgia

I was still smarting from the disappointment of 1986 when Mother announced one day: 'OK, that's it. Next year you are going off to boarding school.' To be honest, I had been asking to be sent to boarding school because it seemed to me then that this was what the smart kids in our neighbourhood did. There were a number of Zulu-medium boarding schools to choose from but, trust Mother and her sense of humour, she decided I would go to a little-known but well-regarded Swazi-medium school in Kangwane, a Swazi-speaking Bantustan on the border with Swaziland. It was an odd choice. I did not speak a word of Swazi and had not studied the language. No matter, Mother decided. Swazi was close enough to Zulu and I would get by. In the event, I lasted just three days at the school. The reasons for my short stay at the school had nothing to do with my language proficiency and everything to do with where I came from.

Having procured the big metal trunk that every boarding-school pupil was supposed to own, and having filled it with tinned food, I arrived at the school to find that, while I and the hundreds of other pupils from Johannesburg and its surrounds had been given places for the year, the headmaster had changed his mind about having so many pupils from eGoli, which is what people who could not be bothered to distinguish between Johannesburg and its surrounds called any place remotely connected to the city. On my second day at the school, the headmaster summoned every kid from Gauteng to assembly and told us we had all been summarily expelled and would be expected to return home by the following day. The headmaster explained that there were too many of us and he could not

Class Warfare

risk having at his school students who had been exposed to class boycotts back in their home towns as we might infect his students with our politics.

This was a strange situation to find oneself in. Our parents had sent us to the boarding school to get us away from the corrupting influence of student politics; the headmaster was sending us home because we were already corrupted. It was as if we were carriers of a virus that could easily spread to his students. The headmaster instructed us to line up outside his office so that we might be reimbursed for the school fees our parents had already paid. There was no room for argument. We all did as told and over the next two days made our way to the local railway station to catch the trains that would take us back to our various townships. Over the years to follow, I was to come across people and discover scholars who took it for granted that to be black and urban – that is, to be from a township – was to be contaminated and not quite the authentic African.

School had already started when I returned home and, with no place to go except Ponego, I duly presented myself early the following week. The Ponego to which I returned was a different school. For one thing, it was under military occupation. There was barbed wire all round the school and its single gate was manned by soldiers who worked in pairs. You had to present your student ID to the soldiers to be let into the school yard. After 8 am, which is when school started, the gate was shut, and the soldiers occupying the school would then patrol the grounds. For some reason, some of the soldiers attached to our school could not get over the fact that one of our teachers was an albino. They would follow him from class to class, peering through the windows to stare at him while he taught. Occasionally, the soldiers would barge into class during lessons for random checks. It was a time when one learnt as much from inside the classroom as from outside.

At Ponego our teachers were a mixed bag. Many obviously cared about why they were there and tried their best to educate us. Our albino teacher, for example, was a study in fortitude as he ignored the taunts of the occupying soldiers peering through the windows and making silly comments about his condition. Other teachers did all they could to help us get a decent schooling. But there were some who obviously did not care. They would show up in class clearly looking the worse for wear from the previous day's drinking. They would spend their lessons making fun of students, talking about sports or whatever caught their fancy. Then there were those who saw in the student protests, which had been continuing virtually non-stop from the 1970s, the end of their world as they knew it.

In a real sense, they were correct. Right through lower and higher primary school, our teachers had exercised corporal punishment as a right. In higher primary school, we had a teacher who carried a suitcase with one thing inside it: a fan belt, for which he even had a nickname. He used it quite liberally, sometimes belting an entire classroom for the infractions of a single student. Other teachers were less creative, using sticks, rulers and waist belts to punish students. Needless to say, school was not particularly popular. In fact, I hated the first four years of my formal education. The only reason I went

Class Warfare

to school was because of my mother. She made it clear to me and the cousins who lived with us that school was the only condition of our staying in her house.

Some of my schoolmates were not so lucky in their choice of mothers. They would play truant from school. But this was Monde Primary School and pupils from Monde did not play truant – or so Mrs M and her teachers told us. As a result the school would organise search parties to round up errant pupils. We would go around the township armed with sticks, stones and, this being Monde, songs. The one we sang the most went something like this: 'ayadoj' amafutha, chicken and rice'. Loosely translated, this means that the fat has run away from a chicken and rice dish, that there is something missing. More often than not, we would find the truant student and drag him kicking and screaming back to school. We would then take him to the assembly, where he would be flogged mercilessly by teachers, who would take turns. It was humiliating and shameful, come to think of it.

Not surprisingly, corporal punishment was one of the main targets of student protests. Students hated the practice. They hated the victimisation it symbolised and the abuse it encouraged. In fact, they made this a key demand of their fight against Bantu education and eventually won the battle when the Department of Education and Training, the state agency responsible for black education under apartheid, announced in the late 1980s that teachers would no longer be allowed to subject students to corporal punishment. Shortly after the announcement was made, one teacher, the mother of a neighbourhood acquaintance, cried in class. 'How am I

Native Nostalgia

going to teach?' she kept asking. She taught Zulu, if I am not mistaken, and had never conducted a class without assaulting at least one student. It was odd.

Seen in another light, the teacher's cry was not altogether surprising. The ban on student beatings meant a further diminution of teacher power over students. It also marked a victory for students in the generational war that was, I believe, a subtext of the 1976 student uprisings. Reading contemporary student accounts of the uprisings, it is clear that part of the motivation among the students was a profound dissatisfaction with their parents. Many students felt that their parents had failed them by not taking the fight to the apartheid government, that parents had acquiesced in their own oppression and that students had been left out to dry by their cowardly carers. Part of this was simply teenage hubris, with the students believing that the struggle against apartheid began with them and that nothing that came before 1976 mattered. The hubris is not unique to South Africans. As Frantz Fanon said, it is the prerogative of youth in each political era to think that the struggle began with them, that previous generations have been a failure. But another part of the explanation for why the 1976 uprisings constituted a generational conflict in the black community stems from the profound lack of appreciation for black protest history displayed by the 1976 protesters.

When Bantu education was introduced in 1954, Katlehong and its predecessor township, Dukathole, were in fact two of the first areas to boycott the new system. ANC volunteers and teachers who refused to teach Bantu education abandoned government schools and formed cultural clubs, using them to conduct schooling for children. Their classes were held under trees and in makeshift rooms. Though the boycott did not last long, it was successful while it lasted. Many of those who took part in the 1976 protests in Soweto, Katlehong and other townships around the country did not know this. That is why they acted as if they were inventing the wheel. In time, however, they came to learn that they were but part of a legacy of struggle. But this did not obscure the generational fissures that were first opened up by the 1976 uprisings and widened by the constant class boycotts of the 1980s.

Students and the youth might have been in the ascendancy in schools and on the streets, but not in our house. My mother reigned supreme. Whatever ideas I picked up outside, I made sure I kept them there. For example, one of the demands of the student movement was for free education. For the movement, this meant the scrapping of school fees. Finally, the government relented in the late 1980s and abolished school fees. Schools were ordered to reimburse students for their fees. You should have seen the parties that ensued as my schoolmates drank their refunds, bought clothes and used the money to show off. It was all at some distance to me, for my mother told me in no uncertain terms that this was her money, that she did not believe in free things and that I was to leave the money where it was. If she ever found out I had asked for a refund, she would throw me on to the street. The threat worked. I must have been the only student not to ask for a refund.

Now that I think about it, it was not simply that my mother did not believe there was nothing for *mahala*. She did not see why protests should come at the expense of education, however hollow that education was. For my mother, who had had to drop out of school as soon as she could write so as to help look after her siblings, education was liberation. Mother was not the only girl in her family to suffer this fate. None of her sisters, except the last-born, was allowed to finish school. They were all yanked out of school as soon as they could write. Each sister, upon reaching a certain age, would be asked to write a letter, in Zulu, to relatives in a far-off place. If the letter received a response, this would be proof enough for my maternal grandfather that his daughter was sufficiently educated. She would then be taken out of school to await marriage.

For my mother, there was no such thing as liberation before education. This is why she did not believe in class boycotts. A proud working-class woman, she might also have objected to the fact that some of those calling for class boycotts were middle-class activists whose kids were safely tucked away in 'multi-racial' private schools where the question of boycotts did not even arise. She must have found it the height of hypocrisy for these men and women to tell us to abandon schools when their own children were being prepared to lead.

To remember my mother's insistence on education is to remember that there were sharp divisions within the black community about how to struggle for freedom. For someone like my mother, whose lack of education had limited the job opportunities available to her, education was key. She did not want her child and those of her siblings to be confined to a life of domestic service. My mother knew many of the local political leaders of her day. She knew also that many were

Class Warfare

college and university graduates. Today there is an often-heard complaint that there is no longer a premium on black success and achievement. It is said that we need black middle-class role models to set an example for the working class. Behind this is the patronising assumption that working-class folks do not know anything about success and hard work. I reject this assumption. That is why when I see my cousins not going to school because they 'do not have anything clean to wear', I see it as a betrayal of my mother and her generation and the struggles they fought to get us educated. They did this despite the venality of apartheid and mean-spiritedness of our social betters. No wonder then that today, when it seems as if township schools are determined to rob young people of their futures, I am nostalgic for a time when education was liberation. A time when our working-class culture valued education, not because our social betters said we ought to but because we knew it was valuable. Like many other things we knew were valuable.

5
The Texture of Money

The working-class culture represented by my mother was a fluid mix of rituals, practices, customs and social orders. This mix governed the way in which adults behaved, families interacted and children were brought up. I call the mix fluid because there was nothing essential about it. Adults did not behave the same way, families did not always interact positively and children were not all brought up identically. There were extramarital affairs, quite a bit of warring between families, and of course children who turned out in ways other than those desired by their parents. There were also families who thought nothing of hanging their dirty linen in public and others for whom discretion was indeed valorous. It was all there. And this being a township, we did not live far from our social betters. The priests, teachers, nurses, clerks and businessmen who made up the local elite lived in the same street as us. They often had the same problems as every other family. In fact, many of the rituals that held our world together were observed by every family in our street. It was the only

Native Nostalgia

way to ensure coexistence.

It is Friday afternoon and my cousins and I are sitting in our lounge shooting the breeze. There is a knock on the door. It is an old woman from the neighbourhood come to tell us that there has been a death in our street. The wife of the man who lives two doors to our right passed away the previous night shortly after complaining about a headache. There are two aspects to the woman's announcement. She wants us to know about the death so that we can pay our condolences to the bereaved family. But she also wants us to prepare a donation for the affected family. We are not the only family the old woman will visit today. She will go to every house in our street and at each place she will greet, ask after the inhabitants' health, say a little something about her health and maybe the weather. Then she will get to the point. The reaction is always the same: shock, amazement and a profuse expression of condolences: 'Ag shame, poor family!'

On the same day the old woman pays us a visit, Mpho, a neighbour's 8-year-old daughter, comes to our front door. The door is open but she knocks anyway. 'Koko,' she says. I am sitting in our lounge writing. 'Kena,' I say. 'Come in.' She walks in. She greets: 'Dumelang.' I respond: 'Aheng.' She asks: 'Is Kamo around?' Kamo is my 4-year-old niece and one of Mpho's best friends in the neighbourhood. Kamo is not around. She has stepped out with her mother. Mpho takes her leave, but before she does so, she thanks me. 'Keya leboha. Salang hantle [Thank you and goodbye].' 'Not a problem,' I say. 'Come back later.' Local schools are closed for their spring break and there is not much for kids to do except frolic in the sun.

The Texture of Money

Mpho returns a few hours later. Again, the same ritual: the knocking, the greeting, the asking and the concluding gratitude and goodbye. Kamo and her mother are still not back. Mpho returns a third time. We follow the same ritual. She is in luck this time; Kamo is back. The two friends go off to play in the street, but not before Mpho says her thank-you and goodbye. Though the ritual sounds elaborate, it takes only a few minutes. An outsider, seeing me and Mpho for the first time, might think that we hardly ever see each other, hence the elaborate ritual. Far from it. Mpho lives right next door and I see her countless times every day.

In the evening, another neighbour comes by. Her observance of the rituals is perfunctory, but it is there nonetheless. She has come to ask if we know about the death. The bereaved family hails from Limpopo. So where is the funeral going to take place? Is it going to happen in the neighbourhood or in Limpopo? This is an important question. The rule is that on the eve of a funeral neighbours visit the bereaved family to slaughter and do what is called *uku-peela* (from the English 'to peel'). The slaughtering is done by the men of the neighbourhood and each man must bring a knife. If, as is increasingly so nowadays, there is no animal slaughtered and the meat is bought from a butcher, the men must show their faces anyway and help with whatever chores need doing. The peeling is done by the women and, again, each woman must bring her own knife. There is always peeling to be done as there are always vegetables served at township funerals. However, none of this is taken for granted. Neighbours will only help those who help others. It has been known for a community to

Native Nostalgia

bury someone but refuse to partake of the food that is always prepared for a funeral. This form of punishment is usually meted out to families who are seen as stingy, antisocial or contrarian. But why the rituals, why the performance?

There are, I think, two parts to the answer. The first is that, as Barrington Moore says, expressions such as 'please' and 'thank you' are 'familiar lubricants of daily social intercourse'. The second part is that, as Theodor Adorno maintains, the rituals that attend greetings, social exchange and community relations suggest the existence of a moral world not governed by means and ends. As Adorno says, 'tenderness between people is nothing other than awareness of the possibility of relations without purpose'. To treat people, including strangers, with kindness is to treat people as ends in themselves, rather than as means to my ends; to treat them with respect and politeness. In my exchanges with Mpho, I recall a younger me. In her politeness, I am reminded of adults saying what good manners it is to greet other people. In Nguni languages, to greet is to acknowledge the existence of the other. 'Sawubona,' we say. I see you. I see your person. But that is not how some observers see it. For some commentators, the rituals of politeness are nothing but a savage practice.

In his masterpiece, *Minima Moralia*, Adorno quotes the following from the Jungian reactionary G.R. Heyer: 'It is a distinguishing habit of people not yet fully formed by civilisation, that a topic may not be directly approached, indeed for some time not even mentioned; rather the conversation must move towards its real object as if by itself, in spirals.' Heyer did not mean this as a compliment. Still, it reminds me

The Texture of Money

of my mother and the social order that existed in our street. There was in our neighbourhood a moral economy of mutual exchange and obligation in which families lent one another money and exchanged food and items such as gardening tools. The rules of this economy were simple. You had to be good for your debt. You had to both give and take in order to stay part of the transactions that defined this economy. What's more, you could not go around gloating that So-and-so owed you some sugar and cooking oil. This was a big no-no.

Another big solecism was that, while you could call gardening tools by name or even ask specifically for them, you could not ask directly for money. Mother would say: 'Son, go to Mrs Buthelezi and ask her for a parcel.' At other times, she would use the word *impahla* – never *imali* (money). So I would go to Mrs Buthelezi's house, knock on the door, go inside, crouch on the floor (you never sat on a chair unless invited to) and, having greeted everyone present, announce my business: 'Mama says to please ask for a parcel.'

Mrs Buthelezi would not respond directly. She would first enquire about everyone at home, ask me about school and then say something about the weather. After a while, Mrs Buthelezi would comment: 'So, your Mom would like a parcel?' The question would be as much to herself as to let you know she had heard you the first time and knew why you were there. If she had a parcel to share, she would get up from her seat, go into her bedroom and return a few minutes later with money neatly folded in a tiny pile. At other times, she would offer profuse apologies, saying she had nothing to share. She would demonstrate her own sorry state by opening up her cupboards to show that, truly, she was not hoarding anything.

In her turn, Mrs Buthelezi would send one of her daughters to ask my mother for a 'parcel'. The same rituals, the greetings, the kneeling on the floor, the extemporaneous conversation, would be gone through before both parties got to the business at hand. These exchanges were governed by a temporal regime all of their own. You could not send a child to ask for a parcel if you needed the cash there and then. The exchanges needed time.

I can't say I fully understood how the value of the 'parcel' was determined. Years later, I asked a neighbour's daughter my age how our parents knew what the value of the parcel was. 'Oh, they would have met and talked beforehand. That's how they knew how much to give. They would have discussed it.' In fact, when it was time to collect on the debt, the same rituals would be performed. You would never go to someone who owed you money and say, 'Pay me back'. Rather, you would go to their house and, after exchanging pleasantries, ask for a parcel. That is what everyone did.

Mia Brandel-Syrier, a Dutch sociologist who studied Katlehong in the 1950s, saw in this social order and philosophy of money a 'non-dualistic worldview' in which there was no qualitative difference between moral and material things. 'The one can be expressed in terms of the other. They are fully interchangeable and in no way opposites.' Brandel-Syrier tended to operate in dualistic terms where things were either Western or African. This dichotomy extended even to her treatment of Katlehong's elite and their experience of social change. For her, things were either white or black

The Texture of Money

and Katlehong's elite were the hapless victims caught in the middle of this sharp divide. Still, she offered good insight into how Katlehong elites spoke about value, wealth and money.

Brandel-Syrier said that the 'meaning of "wealth" in traditional Bantu culture has not yet been fully explored by social anthropologists'. She suggested that there was a 'mystic-organic-procreative' meaning given to the idea of wealth in 'Bantu original cultures' and that we saw this in words such as *impahla*, which is, as I have already said, Zulu for parcel. Quoting other thinkers, Brandel-Syrier commented: 'Clearly, there is in all these interpretations a common denominator. Man's most important tangible possessions, and supremely: money, wealth, cash, which are the modern form of cattle and kin, are the visible manifestations of his true inner worth, that whereby his real (communal) self becomes defined.'

We do not have to go along with Brandel-Syrier's claims about Bantu cultures. But we should take seriously the conclusion she drew from her study: 'My own impression from studying urban life is that much of the older meaning still remains and now colours Black attitudes to money, cash, wealth, property and possessions.' In Katlehong there was certainly a connection between the use of the word 'parcel' to refer to money and that to refer to cattle. My conclusion from this is that the social order which existed in our street was part of the profit economy but followed a different moral logic. According to this logic, borrowing and lending money did not diminish a person's worth. A person was always worth a lot more than the value of his or her possessions. I believe this is the point Adorno was trying to get at with his commentary on Heyer's claims. The trouble with the profit economy for Adorno was that it corrupted humans, instrumentalised social relations and turned individuals into means and ends. 'The practical orders of life, while purporting to benefit man, serve in a profit economy to stunt human qualities, and the further they spread the more they sever everything tender. For tenderness between people is nothing other than awareness of the possibility of relations without purpose ...' According to Adorno, the profit economy killed all possibility of relations that had no obvious end in sight. People could no longer relate with no set outcome in mind. The philosophy of money in my street was, at its best, not limited to what one person could get from another.

At the centre of the social order underpinned by this philosophy was money. However – and this takes us back to Brandel-Syrier's study – money here had a value that went beyond its form as a commodity. That is why you could not simply walk into a person's house and ask for R100. To do this would be to devalue their worth, to dehumanise them. That is why even the lender could not gloat about the amount of money she lent. She knew that individuals did not stop being human simply because they owed you money.

I do not mean to invest this social order with a political agency it might not have had. Families in our neighbourhood participated in this moral economy because, well, that is what the community did. I call it a social order because it governed relations in our street. I see it also as an order because it had within it a logic that was not limited to exchange relations. As Adorno said in response to Heyer, 'the straight line is now

The Texture of Money

regarded as the shortest distance between two people, as if they were points.' Though Adorno was complaining about Western society, his arguments also hold for my society. The examples of my mother and her friends prove that there were people who, while fully enmeshed in a capitalist economy, also carved out autonomous spaces within it. In refusing to treat each other as means, my mother and her contemporaries were living out Adorno's concerns. They believed in a world where old-fashioned courtesies still had their place. Time might have been money for some people but not for my mother – at least not always. This is not to say they existed in the 'there and then' of tradition, as opposed to the 'here and now' of modernity. Rather, they sought in their imperfect ways to see humans in their fullness.

Lending and borrowing parcels from each other were not the only features of Katlehong's social order. There was also the collection of moneys for bereaved families. For reasons never fully explained to me, Mother was the one in charge of the collection of these moneys in our street. Each time there was a death nearby, the affected family would first put ash on its windows and then send out announcements to every house in the neighbourhood. The same day mourners would start showing up, visiting the family to hear what had happened to *umufi* (the departed), and to commiserate with those left behind. The bereaved family would usually clear one room in their house of every piece of furniture except for a mattress. Relatives of the departed would take turns sitting on the mattress, telling mourners what had happened to the dead person. Never mind that everyone knew how he or she died.

Native Nostalgia

The story would have to be told again each time a new group of mourners came in.

Unlike in other cultures, the family of the dead would have to provide food for mourners. Every person who came through the yard would be served tea with homemade biscuits. That is what everyone did. If there was electricity, the bereaved family would turn off all the lights in the room with the mattress and use only candles. A friend says the practice of stripping a room bare and leaving only a mattress on the floor is an act of necessity that was turned into a cultural practice by the passage of time. He says that because early urban houses were small, the bereaved family had to clear the main bedroom to make way for the mourners they knew would come. Out of this grew the tradition of sitting on a mattress. There are other rituals connected to death and mourning that some would swear are African and timeless. One of these is the wearing of a black, blue or green habit by the widow to symbolise her loss. Elders swear by these practices. But as W.G. Sebald shows, they were once common in Europe.

In the main bedroom where the bereaved family received mourners, a candle would mark the spot where every mourner left a little donation for the family of the dead person. Usually, there would be a book on the floor in which mourners used to record their donation. In this way, the whole street knew who had donated and who had not.

As soon as a death was announced, my mother would spring into action. While she kept the books recording the street's donations to bereaved families, I would be the one to knock on every house to collect donations. People almost always gave

The Texture of Money

money. The last thing anyone wanted was to have a death in the family and be without community support. In fact, to this day, there is nothing worse in a township than a poorly attended funeral. Everyone wants a good send-off – even if they do not always get a good death. So I would go from house to house, telling people that such-and-such a family had had a death and asking people to give what little they could. There was no set figure for the donation. For me, the positive side-effect of all this was that I grew up knowing pretty much every family in our street. I knew who was an insider and who was an outsider. I knew which family was consistent with its contributions and which one tardy. It was through these rounds that I was introduced to the various characters who peopled our streets.

This social order bears writing about because townships tend to be seen as zones of deprivation that can only ever be defined in a negative sense, in terms of what they do not possess. In the telling of most histories, townships are poor places, full of poor people who often make poor choices in life. They are spaces where only the fit survive. They desperately 'need' development and lack any order. But, as scholars such as Gillian Hart, Henri Lefebvre and David Harvey point out, there is nothing 'natural' about space or time. In fact these categories of measurement are also products of everyday practices and they are always constitutive of human exchange.

In some ways, the predominant way of thinking about townships takes as its starting point the fact that they were originally intended to serve as dormitories of labour. However, it would be wrong to think of townships only in terms of their economic function. As Hart says, we must avoid reducing everything to the economic in the final analysis. We must reject economism but without losing sight of the importance of exchange and labour relations in the making of societies and the shaping of individual and collective consciousnesses. Says Hart: 'Rejecting economism emphatically does *not* [her emphasis] mean neglecting the powerful role of economic forces and relations but rather recognising that economic practices and struggles over material resources and labour are always and inseparably bound up with culturally constructed meanings, definitions, and identities, and with the exercise of power, all as part of historical processes.' In the case of Katlehong, this means recognising the fact that while townships are predominantly working-class areas, they are in fact multi-class neighbourhoods. It also means acknowledging that material relations do not determine everything.

In calling for the rejection of economism, Hart alerts us to another important dimension to the argument under way here, namely that the hegemony of the powerful is fragile. By hegemony is meant the strategies by which ruling elites naturalise their rule by co-opting the ruled and absorbing class contradictions and transforming these into the constitutive elements of the body politic. Hart's claim that hegemony is fragile allows us to see the salience of Michel Foucault's insight that power implicates in its exercise those over whom it is exercised. It also helps us understand resistance to the ruling classes, or why it takes the form it often does, where there is no full-scale revolt but only minor acts of resistance. These acts of resistance are possible because the dominance

The Texture of Money

of ruling classes is never absolute. Such acts do not always take a political form and may be expressed through culture and plays on language. This is yet another indication of the weaknesses inherent in economism. In the last instance, putting everything down to the determination of the economic leaves us well short of a full understanding of how individuals live and why they do the things they do. As Hart says: 'In other words, while material conditions and economic power relations define broad conditions of existence, they do not in any unilateral and automatic fashion guarantee the specific forms of ongoing material/cultural struggles or the formation of political identities.'

Hart also brings us to one of the key but implicit motivations for this book: the role of imagination in the production of space. To give a practical example, Katlehong is more than just a township made up of houses and basic amenities. Katlehong is also a world that exists in the imagination, a world where the metaphorical is as important as the material. This is true of every space inhabited by human beings in the world. As Hart says: 'The production of space also implies the production of meanings, concepts, and consciousness about space (or space–time) that are inseparably linked to its physical production through situated practices.'

We cannot deal with these meanings without engaging with the role of memory in the production of space and time. If space and time are categories of measurement that are, at the same time, mutually constitutive of human exchange, if space and time are not 'natural' entities but socially produced products of the human imagination, there are serious implications for

Native Nostalgia

how we think about history. This is for the simple reason that to think about history is to think about a given place in a given time. It is also to think about memory as a constitutive element of history. What, after all, are our memories if they are not of given places in a given time?

To ask this question is to flag a problem that is never far from the surface when memories are invoked, namely how to come to terms with nostalgia. This has added significance for my book because I am dealing with an urban formation whose history is inextricably linked with that of apartheid. The South African journalist Tiisetso Makube once asked: 'How could nostalgia not be an important and concomitant part of the architecture of our national psyche?' Now, if you think that townships are zones of deprivation and are nothing but vast labour camps, how can you remember such places with longing? How can you be nostalgic for such places? But nostalgic about townships most people are. We even have a phenomenon called 'living in the township, sleeping in the suburbs'. This is a phenomenon whereby young black professionals who have bought houses in formerly white suburbs spend their waking lives in townships. They only go to their new houses to sleep. The explanation often given is that there is 'no life' in the suburbs and that they don't know their suburban neighbours.

This phenomenon makes sense only if one understands that not everything we did in townships was a reaction to white oppression. Townships were (and are) dynamic places where attention to local detail (the music, the colours, the sounds, the smells) is what gave Katlehong, in my case, its distinct flavour and made it possible for me to tell it apart from, say,

The Texture of Money

the neighbouring township of Thokoza.

Townships also induce nostalgia because they have always had people with sufficient cultural imagination to show that township life is not all doom and gloom. Listen to the music. Think of the different dance styles with which we grew up. Cast your mind back to the street games we played which heralded the change in seasons: black *mampatile* in winter; kites in spring; tops and marbles in autumn; and boom and *bhathi* in summer. This is not to mention the role that our elders played (not always successfully) in teaching us wrong from right; the values (both positive and negative) we learnt from observing parents, neighbours, siblings squabbling – or the damage done by drink and crime to families. To be nostalgic is not to wear rose-tinted glasses but to appreciate township life in its complexity.

It seems to me that in a time when to think positively about black life under apartheid is, as Walter Benjamin would say, to 'brush history against the grain', the act of remembering has itself acquired a political meaning. To remember is a political act, for it means to refuse to buy into the annihilation of the moral agents whose primary world was and still is the township. By no means is the act of remembering, the work of memory, itself an innocent act. It comes against the backdrop of what Andreas Huyssen calls a 'memory boom'. Huyssen says that we need both the past and the future in order to come to terms with the present and to effect the work of political imagination that is a prerequisite for the creation of a new world. But he is also aware of the field of discourse on which the work of memory is taking place. Huyssen says: 'Whatever the specific content of the many contemporary debates about history and memory may be, underlying them is a fundamental disturbance not just of the relationship between history as objective and scientific, and memory as subjective and personal, but of history itself and its premises. *At stake* [his emphasis] in the current history–memory debate is not only a disturbance of our notions of the past, but a fundamental crisis in our imagination of alternative futures.'

We can see this 'fundamental crisis in our imagination of alternative futures' in the way townships are depicted in government policy: as docile recipients of state largesse and service delivery. This is not only patronising, it is anti-politics as well. There is also a tendency to treat townships as places of trauma and township life itself as a sad and traumatic experience. That, too, is patronising, for it turns township residents into perpetual victims. Speaking of the place of trauma in memory and history, Huyssen says:

> It has been all too tempting to some to think of trauma as the hidden core of all memory. After all, both memory and trauma are predicated on the absence of that which is negotiated in memory or in the traumatic symptom. Both are marked by instability, transitoriness, and structures of repetition. But to collapse memory into trauma … would unduly confine our understanding of memory, marking it too exclusively in terms of pain, suffering and loss. It would deny human agency and lock us into compulsive repetition. Memory, whether individual or generational, political or public, is always more than only the prison house of the past.

The Texture of Money

I want to riff off Huyssen to say that, in collapsing the memory of the past into trauma, we limit our understanding of South Africa's past and of the country's townships. Once we do that, we mark townships 'too exclusively in terms of pain, suffering and loss'. It is the singular feature of human beings that even amid the depths of despair they do not lose their sense of being. There is always more to life than the suffering that individuals are subjected to at any given time. Again, to point this out is not to ignore the serious problems that exist in townships. I merely want to insist, with W.E.B. DuBois, that we don't confuse individuals with the problems they face. As Huyssen says: 'The issue ... is not the loss of some golden age of stability and permanence. The issue is rather the attempt, as we face the very real processes of time–space compression, to secure some continuity within time, to provide some extension of lived space within which we can breathe and move.'

To remember, then, is a political act. It is not, however, to articulate the past 'the way it really was'. As Benjamin says: 'It means to seize hold of a memory as it flashes up at a moment of danger.' To write positively about memories of a township life is not to hanker after 'some golden age of stability and permanence'. But it does mean seizing hold of memories of the past without denying the agency of the individuals who live in townships. How, then, shall we do this? Huyssen suggests the following: 'In the meantime we have to ask: how should even local, regional, or national memories be secured, structured, and represented? Of course, this is a fundamentally political question about the nature of the public sphere, about democracy and its future, about the changing shape of nationhood, citizenship and identity.'

I cannot emphasise this enough. In securing memories of my township, I want to alert us to the role that townships must play in the constitution of the public sphere, the evolution of nationhood, citizenship and identity in post-apartheid South Africa. Lefebvre says no revolution can succeed if it does not reconstitute space. We must secure township memories because they are, as Tiitsetso Makube says, a constitutive part of the national psyche – and it is, quite frankly, impossible to think of South Africa without townships. This is not to ignore the real problems that exist in townships. These problems can and must be solved. But we do ourselves no favours by seeing townships only as problem areas, zones of lack, that have nothing to give to the constitution of a democratic South Africa. Rather we need to recuperate a positive definition of townships. Achille Mbembe says:

> Almost ten years after the end of apartheid, we have very few postliberation ethnographies of everyday life in the township. We have even fewer academic or theoretical reflections on its place in the city, its rhythms and senses. That the township both is and is not urban, that it is proximate to the city while at its margins, and that city and township are inextricably linked under apartheid – all these points are incontestable. So is the fact that the township still suffers from a lack of basic amenities, even as it exhibits the extremes of poverty and wealth characteristic of the city. Nevertheless, we are left with a negative definition of this highly syncretic

The Texture of Money

urban formation that is integral to city life in South Africa and deeply embedded in the nation's social imaginary and political unconscious.

In addition to posing a challenge to the master narrative of black homogeneity, this book is also a modest and imperfect contribution towards attempts to set the terms for an ethnography of a township. I would consider it a success if it gave a positive definition of Katlehong that was also cognisant of the challenges the township continues to face. It would have succeeded if it yanked the township out of the web of exceptionalism and marginalisation in which townships in general are caught. There is no better way to strip difference of its mystique than to deal directly with practices of everyday life on their own terms while also linking them to the wider world. While material and economic power relations, which differ from place to place, might define broad conditions of existence, they are not all there is to human life. As Mbembe says of the township, 'although invented by the apartheid state, [it] was and continues to be produced well beyond the apartheid moment.'

It might be tempting for some to read this to mean that townships are nothing but places of splendour, heavens on earth. That is most definitely not the case. While people have lived and continue to live in townships in all sorts of creative ways, townships are not without their problems. In fact, townships can sometimes get on one's nerves.

6
The Sense of Township Life

There is no telling when a township will get on your nerves. It could be in August, when the promise of spring comes covered in dusty winds that sting the eye and stick in the throat. It could be in the dog days of December when boomboxes and gumba gumbas set off a sonic wave that drowns streets in a sea of music. It could also be at dawn when the crowing of a neighbour's cock and the barking of a stray dog vie with the horn of a minibus taxi touting for early-morning business to create a sleep-killing racket. To live in a township is to live in a world of the senses. It is to inhabit a world in which one's nerves are often exposed: on edge about whether the stepping stone you see ahead of you in the dark as you perform yet another high-jump over a grey sewage stream is indeed a rock and not one of those rats which the tabloids swear are the size of cats. To say a township will get on your nerves is not to say the status of township residents is, like that of the Sartrean native, a nervous condition. Rather, it is to point out that here, too, people see, smell, taste, touch and hear. They

Native Nostalgia

cannot do otherwise. As the author of *A Natural History of the Senses*, Diane Ackerman, says, 'There is no way in which to understand the world without first detecting it through the radar-net of our senses.'

The tastes, textures, smells, sights and sounds that issue from a township might make an immediate impression on one's nerves. After all, there is no mistaking the smell of sewage. But it takes a while for some of these sensations to get on one's nerves: a whole season in the case of the harsh Highveld winter whose severity always catches everyone by surprise. One needs to be in a township in July, the cold heart of winter in South Africa, to know that the Brits are not the only ones obsessed with talk about the weather. Township residents can talk about nothing else at this time of year. How can they when the dew point seems to have dropped so low that winter feels as if it starts right *emkantsheni*, in the marrow? When no layers of clothing suffice to keep the cold at bay? When no township house is warm enough and no record can testify to what always feels like the coldest winter in living memory? But the lament is seasonal. It withers with the onset of spring and its profusion of colour in September. You certainly won't hear it during summer and its cacophony of sound. But like a perennial flower that is forever present, even when it does not always show itself, the moan returns the moment a new winter season starts, with township residents swearing on their mothers and the cross of Jesus ('Umam' isiphambano!') that they never knew it could get so cold in Gauteng. 'Yo, we didn't know it could be this nasty!' But pay them no attention, for you will hear the same groan next year, and the one after that.

The Sense of Township Life

However, if winter is the harshest season for Highveld township dwellers, August must be the cruellest month. The harmattans that seem to blow in from everywhere do not so much coat everything in layers of dust as grate against the nerves as nothing else can. In fact, it is at this time of year that the pay-off line beloved of so many washing soap adverts – to give you the whitest whites – becomes a dirty joke. Pity the resident – and that's pretty much everybody – who has to hang her washing on an outside line. Pity, too, the fool dumb enough to perm his hair in August when dust sticks to the grease applied to such hairstyles like, well, dirt on oil. We won't even mention those with a fetish for clean surfaces. As township lingo has it, 'U-clean unga-cleananga ngo-August [You are forever cleaning in August].' Yet we can't blame it all on August.

It is a custom in many township homes for a woman, especially a newly-wed, to prove her worth by sweeping the family yard. If you go for a jog between 5 am and 6 am, you will see armies of women, doeks on their heads and blankets wrapped round their waists, sweeping up a dust storm as they prove their worth. The storms generated daily by these traditional armies are of course nothing compared to the cruelties of August. But one can't help wondering if the August winds are nature's revenge for the scrubbing to which the topsoil is subjected. Revenge, perhaps, like that paid by the skin of a woman whose face is scarred by *imemezi*, the skin-lightening topical agent that leaves its users with *amashubaba* – cracked cheeks that look like the barren earth of a township yard.

Native Nostalgia

To say a township will get on your nerves is to acknowledge that there is a lot about a township experience that grates. However, it would be to limit one's sense of a township, one's understanding of it, to reduce this experience simply to the smell of burst sewerage pipes, the noise of township dogs and taxis, and the tastes of *kasie* food. It would be to take a part, as impermanent as that may be, for the whole. It is not the case that every township woman uses skin-lightening creams or sweeps her yard every day, that there is always a burst sewerage pipe or that townships are forever noisy. This is not to suggest that such things should be ignored. But for far too long these aspects, not to mention the hypervisible problems of poverty, crime and disease, have come to define township life in ways that do nothing to educate us about the practices of everyday life in townships. In a sense, to define townships in terms of their problems is to reduce township residents themselves to problems – instead of seeing them as people *with* problems, some of which are personal and others collective: just like every human being on earth, in fact.

This book is inspired by the senses. But this is because that is the only way, it seems to me, in which one can write feelingly about townships – in human terms. By insisting on the five senses as its point of departure, this book seeks to displace what passes for common sense in how we think about townships. It is all too easy to look at a township and see only monotonous rows of matchbox houses; to smell in a winter evening nothing but the sulphuric smog of coal-fired braziers; to taste in township fare such as *amagwinya* only artery-clogging fat of dubious provenance; to hear in the din of a

The Sense of Township Life

minibus taxi nothing but the apparent disorder of a township and its inhabitants; and to feel when touching the roughcast wall of a four-roomed 'matchbox' only the 'dirt and disease and depression of the spirit in that area'. That, as I say, is all too easy.

Far more difficult is to go behind our common sense of what a township is to discover what Achille Mbembe calls the 'rhythms and senses' of the place. We could call townships impoverished, poor, underprivileged and lacking in social services. We could describe them as 'warehouses for labour' or, a personal favourite, 'previously disadvantaged areas for previously disadvantaged individuals', as many writers and thinkers do. But that litany of emotive adjectives does not tell us anything about how the people who reside in the 300-odd spaces designated as black townships in South Africa actually live. It does not tell us what it is like to live in a township, given its complex place in South Africa's political economy. It definitely does not enlighten us about the place's rhythms and rituals and how inhabitants are constantly making sense of their worlds and giving meaning to their lives. It is not surprising that township inhabitants do this. What is surprising, however, is that a lot of writing on townships does not acknowledge this elementary fact.

How, then, does one develop a new sense of a township? What does it mean to reflect on its 'rhythms and senses'? Answering these questions means diving deep into the well of personal and collective memory to remember the smells, sights, sounds and other sensations that make townships – as heterogeneous as these places are – unique. This is not to suggest, say, that all townships sound the same or that they all smell the same. The sounds one hears in Mkhuhlu, a predominantly Shangaan-speaking township outside Hazyview, on the western border of the Kruger National Park, are different from what one hears in Xhosa-dominated Langa, outside Cape Town. Nor is it to say that all townships look alike. The flat, yellowy, desert townships of the Northern Cape look nothing like the verdant hilly locations of KwaZulu-Natal.

However, while human beings may not smell the same, see the same or even taste the same, the point is that we all depend on the 'radar-net of our senses' to find our place in the world. Human beings can all relate to the fact that the world comes to us through the five senses we all share in common. So, framing this book in terms of the senses is, in effect, to put what follows here in human terms, to make the case for a new understanding of townships in a way that everyone can potentially follow.

Here is how that new way of sensing a township might develop. Let us take our eyes. It is all too easy to look at a township and see only a row of squat houses that look depressingly alike. That, in fact, is how townships are often depicted. But there is nothing innocent about the 'look' we give townships. This is for the simple reason that while sight is without doubt one of the most important human faculties, it takes more than just the physiological contraption we term the eye to do what an American president memorably termed 'the vision thing'. As Diane Ackerman says, 'To taste or touch your enemy or your food, you have to be unnervingly close to it. To smell or hear it, you can risk being farther off.' But

The Sense of Township Life

vision 'can travel across time' and cover distances we can't even smell over. The sense of sight gives us a conceptual mobility that adds to what is already a formidable human capacity to travel. In fact, Ackerman says, 'It may even be that abstract thinking evolved from our eyes' elaborate struggle to make sense of what they saw.' This means that sight is both a physiological activity and a function of the mind. In other words, we see as much with our eyes as we do with our brains. But brains are not innocent organs. They are also conditioned by quirks of nature, accidents of birth and the owner's material circumstances, among other things.

In the case of a township and the way we see it, what is apparent to a viewer (that what she has in front of her is row upon row of unimaginative houses on dusty streets) may be as much a function of what her brain has been taught to 'see' as what she sees in front of her. However, to see townships purely through a 'tainted' brain is to reduce to an abstract entity what is in fact a complex urban formation. I have only to think back to the township streets on which I grew up. Where an outsider might have noticed nothing but dreary uniformity, I would have seen that some houses regularly wore fresh paint while others did not, that some gardens boasted marigolds, red roses and euphorbias while others did not. I would have seen, too, that while most houses in our streets had only Kikuyu grass, one neighbour in particular had the kind of grass some people insisted was similar to that laid at Wimbledon.

As sociologists point out, the (social) eye is trained to see things a certain way. So, where outsiders might have seen in a township a homogeneous empty space peopled by interchangeable black bodies, I grew up seeing bodies that sounded and looked like the different social classes, ethnicities and genders that inhabited a township. I could see in what people wore, for example, that they were of a particular class. But one needed a particular kind of common sense for this: a common sense that knew how to read township 'Jewish', which is what fashion was and is called in townships; in other words, a common sense that was alive to the vast differences that lurked behind the apparent dull uniformity of a township. These differences cut across gender, class, ethnicity and many other things besides. In some ways, the outsider's vision of these differences was hidden from view by both an apartheid ideology that often treated black people as an undifferentiated mass, on the one hand, and a liberation movement that almost always depicted blacks as indistinguishable heroic 'masses of our people', on the other. Both visions obscured from sight the differences that made black life interesting and complex.

But sight is not the only sense through which we make sense of township life. Human beings always smell and yet they can't describe a smell to someone who has not smelt it. Though we can only share our pleasure or distaste over a smell, we can't share the sensation sparked by the smell with someone who has not been subjected to similar sensations. But that is not all. As Ackerman says, we may smell with every breath, but smell is a mute sense, 'the one without words'. We need light to see, our mouths to taste, our skin to touch, and ears to hear sounds. But we need only be alive to smell. We 'smell always and with every breath'.

How does a township smell? One could take the lazy option

The Sense of Township Life

and focus only on the burst sewerage pipes which, while not a standard feature of townships by any means, are common enough for people to talk about them. Or one could take the more difficult route and think back, as I often do, to the first time I smelt teargas: somewhat bitter, somewhat peppery – but never pleasant. That is how I would describe the smell of teargas.

Because smell is, as Ackerman says, a mute sense, 'the one without words', I would have to begin the recollection of my first experience of teargas by pointing out that the smell came to me in the form of a sharp, piercing scream that always springs to mind when I grapple with the meaning of apartheid. It was the early 1980s and the scream was uttered by a young woman in a neighbourhood not far from my Grandmother P's house. I had gone to the local shops to buy bread or something and was walking back when I heard the scream. The woman must have been upwind of me because, as I later discovered, her scream came as she was overcome by fumes from a teargas canister fired by a policeman. The shooting must have been a bit of a lark because it was a Saturday and the township was, politically speaking, quiet. Cops and soldiers often did that: fire teargas canisters into tents where old women were holding prayer meetings or halls where funerals were under way – just to see people choke on the fumes. Once, my mother was at a night vigil, and just as the congregation was singing *Nkosi Sikelel' iAfrika*, a military patrol drove by. The young soldiers did not ask any questions. They fired teargas into the tent and told the old women at the vigil to disperse. They did not care that this was a religious ceremony. They cared only that the

Native Nostalgia

women were singing *Nkosi Sikelel' iAfrika*, which was the anthem of the revolution.

Anyway, when I first heard the woman's scream I thought someone had been attacked. But it did not take long for the wind to turn and for me to get a taste of what had made the woman scream so. As people on the streets ran into neighbourhood yards to wet their T-shirts and hats to use as masks, I ran home half-blind, unsure what had hit me. It was only when I got home and told my family what had happened that the elders nodded knowingly. They had each been through a similar experience in their lives at some point. That, for me, was a smell of townships.

But teargas was not a regular feature of township life. Townships did not always smell of a pungent, peppery odour. There were times when they smelt of grilled meat, burning plastic and many things in between. You could not and cannot say that a township smells like this or like that. But you could say – and that is the point – that a township was and is a world of smells. A world, in other words, of the senses. These senses included textures and tastes such as that of *i-quarter*, actually a Gauteng corruption of the famous bunny chow. The difference is that whereas the bunny chow is a quarter loaf stuffed with lamb, beef, chicken or vegetable curry, *i-quarter*, which gets its name from the size of the bread used, is stuffed with fries, atchar, sausages, cheese and whatever else the maker can squeeze inside the bread. Doctors recommend the anti-diarrhoeal Imodium to stop a running tummy. They should prescribe township quarters instead. Nothing stuffs up, literally, a tummy like *i-quarter*. But that is just one of many township tastes.

The Sense of Township Life

We may close our eyes or squeeze our noses to neutralise our senses of sight and smell. But there is nothing one can do to shut out the noise that becomes a township in summer. When tributaries of noise flow from every front door to create a virtual sea of music, the only thing one can do is dive into the sea and enjoy the music as best one can. I discovered this the hard way in December 2008. A neighbour with a powerful set of speakers was playing his music at full blast. You could hear the music from everywhere: there was no getting away from it. He was playing the O'Jays. 'At least the bastard has a decent taste in music,' I complained to cousin S. 'Oh-ho,' replied cousin S. 'That is my CD he is playing. I had to give it to him after he bombarded the street with the same CD of monotonous house music for weeks on end. This way, he gets to play music that we can at least appreciate, even if we are forced to listen to it.'

I grew up next door to a shebeen and am sometimes tempted to agree with claims that sound is the predominant sense in a township. There were certainly times in my childhood when I knew popular songs, not because I was 'into' music as such, but because our shebeen neighbours played them to death. That was one of the many things that made a shebeen a shebeen. I also grew up in a neighbourhood with many independent African churches that were fond of *imilindelo*, weekend night vigils, and a house full of sangomas, where the ancestral drums would sound almost every night, as spirits were called and ancestors propitiated. But I would be lying if I said it was all sound and fury. There were certainly times when my street and neighbourhood were quiet. This was especially true in the time when it seemed every adult had a job and every kid was at school. That is why many of us hated dodging: playing truant from school. It was boring on the streets during the day. They were quiet and there was nothing to do. Better to be at school where you at least had something to keep you occupied.

In placing the five senses at the centre of this book, I do not intend to privilege certain sounds, sights, smells, textures and tastes above others. To do that would be to commit the same mistake I see committed all the time in literary treatments of townships, namely to pretend that a township is experienced in the same way by every person who passes through it. Townships have never been static spaces. They have always been dynamic and creative arenas whose very meaning has been subject to contestation. The way my childhood friends and I experienced our street was very different from the way our parents walked the same streets. There was also a difference in how the employed and the jobless experienced a township. To put this in other words, people who woke up early to commute to work and only returned home after sunset felt and saw a township differently from those who did not have jobs and spent the day chasing the sun around the yard, as we say in township lingo.

Then there were the gender differences. In fact, one could argue that if Friday was a men's day on township streets, Thursdays and Sundays were women's days. Thursday was when women's church groups, *abomama bomanyano*, got together. Sunday was when churches (most of which were dominated by women) and women's burial societies got together. This made perfect sense. Saturday was a day for

The Sense of Township Life

doing the laundry and getting groceries; Sunday was the day for everything else. I do not mean to suggest that women did not go out on Fridays: they certainly did. However, in doing so, they partook of a leisure economy that was coded essentially as male.

This was ironic when you consider the fact that most shebeens were and are run by women. As various scholars have pointed out, Johannesburg, like Kimberley before it, was conceived of as a male space. There was no room for women. But many women carved a space for themselves in these urban areas and in the townships that followed them through the beer-brewing business. This is how a sizeable number of African women secured their freedom in these non-traditional and freewheeling spaces. This did not mean, however, that women could enter spaces such as shebeens without picking up sexist baggage, as it were. To this day, women who frequent shebeens, drink beer and smoke are considered 'loose', *straatmeisies* (Afrikaans for women of the street). That is why Friday, which is when most people go to shebeens, can be described as a men's day.

Not surprisingly, shebeens did not all look alike or even play the same music. Some served food; others did not. Some had a dress code; many did not. Some enforced an age limit; many did not (this in fact became a serious problem when schooling was disrupted by protests and state repression in the late 1970s and early 1980s). They certainly did not cater to the same clientele. There were shebeens that catered to the government clerks, teachers, nurses and other public servants who made up the lower black middle class. Yet there were yet other joints, taverns, which served only doctors and business people; some which catered to labourers and other members of the working class; and, finally, those that served *imbamba*, a brew so potent – thanks to its ingredients of carbolic soap, battery acid, methylated spirits and stale bread – that it gave its users an ashen look that couldn't be mistaken for anything else. Later on, *imbamba* got so ugly its brewers and drinkers took to calling it *takunyisa*, which is Shangaan for 'I'll fuck you up' or 'I'll make you shit yourself'. And that is exactly what the brew did.

But the fact that those who drank in working-class shebeens and *imbamba* haunts seemed to constitute the majority of drinkers in a township should not blind us to the fact that shebeens were just one of many markers of social distinction in a township. There were many others, such as the type of house one lived in, the car one drove, the church one worshipped at, the burial society one belonged to, the pastimes one followed and the places where one shopped. Township residents knew this. In the case of Katlehong, they also knew what your neighbourhood said about you. For example, people did not need to be told that a section of the township called the Administration Block was where state clerks, teachers, doctors and other professionals lived. It also did not take a genius to know that Khalambazo (the place of wailing axes) was a rough working-class part of Nhlapo Section. I write this fully aware that these are not pure descriptions. As Henri Lefebvre remarks, there is a spatial economy that determines the way people describe a neighbourhood as 'safe', 'quiet' or 'rough'. This book seeks to confront such descriptions and to

The Sense of Township Life

call into question this spatial economy. It does this by detailing snippets of township life in a way that illustrates the richness of that life. This is not to valorise township experience or to offer a defence of townships. To corrupt Marx, the job of a writer should not simply be to describe townships but to change the way such descriptions are given. Mine is, then, a modest endeavour.

In truth, to make sense of a South African township is in effect to make sense of the black urban experience. It is to make sense of social and political sensations that began in the nerves. Hear it in the names that the earliest African migrants gave to Gauteng, the place of gold, and its surrounds. Gauteng was Kwandongaziyaduma, the place of resounding walls, or Kwanyam' ayipheli kuphel' amaziny' endoda, the place of excess, where the only thing finite was a man's teeth, not the meat he could eat every day. Johannesburg, the commercial and cultural capital of Gauteng, was Jozi Maboneng, the city of lights. As a famous Radio Zulu presenter of the 1980s put it, Gauteng was Kwamtanami wendelephi na? (roughly translated, it means 'Who knows which man and which of Gauteng's many dens of iniquity have claimed my daughter?').

The point is not whether these descriptions were accurate. That, in fact, is beside the point. Rather, what matters here is that all these descriptions spoke of the new urban experience as an experience of the senses. They spoke of it as a series of new sounds, smells, textures, tastes and sights. The urban experience worked itself in the senses. It was, to put it another way, felt – a felt experience. It is not often that writers and thinkers take seriously the descriptions that Africans gave of their feelings, their sense of what it meant to be urban. More common is to treat Africans as hapless victims of a mechanical process of proletarianisation. I do not dispute the profound changes that took place in southern Africa as more and more Africans entered the market economy. However, I question historical accounts of this process that treat it only and simplistically as a materialist development. The point is urbanisation had a sensuous as well as a material dimension to it. It was as much about material conditions as it was about how people felt it and, dare we say, felt about it.

We know, for example, that sections of African society felt differently about the new urban experience. If traditional African society dreaded losing its young to the anonymity of the urban jungle, sections of white South Africa feared getting lost in the same jungle as the natives. The urban native evoked fears among some white South Africans that, unless something was done to check black urban migration, hordes of disease-bearing tribesmen and women would swamp them. In fact, the majority of the black urban settlements we call townships today grew out of a deep sense of (white) dread that government was losing control over black urbanisation. There was, among the white establishment, a sense that there were way too many natives in South Africa's fast-growing cities and towns with no reliable footing in either the tradition represented by the chief and the rural homestead or the modernity of the city, with its multiple sensations. This was the black peril. This is the fear that lay at the heart of the National Party's apartheid programme.

Very few thinkers cared much for the new urban African

The Sense of Township Life

either. As Karl Polanyi, in one of his most unsavoury moments, said: 'The Kaffir of South Africa, a noble savage, than whom none felt socially more secure in his native kraal, has been transformed into a human variety of half-domesticated animal dressed in the "unrelated, the filthy, the unsightly rags that not the most degenerated white man would wear," a nondescript being, without self-respect or standards, veritable human refuse.' If Polanyi's observation echoed Joseph Conrad's description in *Heart of Darkness* of the half-man, half-dog figure who is the mute subject of Kurtz's twisted mind, it was probably because Polanyi wanted to call on the same sense of fear of the corrupted native evoked by Conrad.

For apartheid thinkers such as G. Marais and R. van der Kooy, the problem of what they quaintly called 'the urban black nation' was indeed a problem of nerves. According to these two men, modernity was such a fast-paced assault on the senses that the urban native could not possibly be expected to cope without help. Marais and Van der Kooy wrote: 'The seriousness of this problem is due: Firstly, to the urban blacks who themselves are in a most difficult stage of their adjustment; the difficulty of adjusting from being tribesmen to becoming city-dwellers. It is the difficulty of adjusting to differences between tribal discipline and individualism, between a subsistence economy and a highly competitive market economy, between African religions and Christianity, between rural security and urban insecurity and between tribal realisation and self-realisation.'

I am not interested per se in pointing out the shallowness of this contrived opposition between a timeless tribal realisation

Native Nostalgia

and a racialised self-realisation. But I am keen to show why my focus on the senses in this book is a serious matter. Here are two examples. In a book published in the 1950s entitled *The Establishment of a Bantu Township*, J.E.W. Mathewson writes knowingly about the cost of establishing a new black location. He says one of the biggest expenses in running a township is the maintenance of a sewerage network. This is because blacks are literally full of shit. Mathewson does not put it in such crude terms but that is precisely what he means. Here is the full quote:

> In the case of Daveyton sewage disposal works, which will serve a township consisting entirely of Bantu residents, a factor which warranted special consideration was that the nature of the Bantu diet, which, being principally carbohydrate in character, such as mealies, is deficient in protein and this necessitates a very much higher consumption of food than that of Europeans who live on a more concentrated diet. In consequence the amount of faecal matter to be treated per capita is greater than that for a mixed township and the capacities of the sludge digestor and sludge drying beds will therefore be greater than that normally provided for a European township.

Mathewson was not joking. As he pointed out in his book, city fathers were spending 50 per cent more money in the township of Daveyton than they were in its white 'parent city' of Benoni. What could be more sensuous than a person's bowel movements, especially when such movements are factors in

The Sense of Township Life

government planning?

The second example is more serious, but it, too, makes the case for why we need to place the senses more directly at the centre of our considerations of South African history. The example is this: Katlehong, the East Rand township that is the setting for the reflections in this book, is known by many today as the site of the brutal wars that nearly derailed South Africa's transition to democracy in the early 1990s. Katlehong was the eye of the violent storm that claimed more than two thousand lives in the area and left thousands injured and hundreds displaced. Incidentally, the violence began as a taxi war between a Zulu-dominated taxi organisation and a new association controlled by township residents. It began, in fact, in May 1990 with the brutal slaying of seven students and one teacher at Katlehong High School, the oldest high school in the township. The Katlehong Civic Association responded to this initial episode with a public meeting attended by about ten thousand residents. The taxi war that occasioned the May meeting was no laughing matter. As the Truth and Reconciliation Commission later found, the war was real and bloody and there were definite material interests behind it (Who controls which taxi route? Who gets to decide who can operate a taxi in the township? How are hostel dwellers to relate to township residents? & etc.). These material interests made the conflict possible, turning neighbour against neighbour in some cases.

But pointing out the material bases of the war is not to forget the 'small' moments (of humour) that punctuated the bloodletting. I am thinking in particular of the grievances

133

that township residents had against (Zulu) taxi drivers and the memorandum they drew up at their meeting that May day. Among the grievances listed in the memorandum were complaints that taxi drivers did not wash, and a demand that they at least use deodorant to make their passengers' journeys bearable. A minor detail for some, but an important issue of nerves for the thousands of commuters who use taxis every day.

7
The Language of Nostalgia

'So, how many languages do you speak?' a person, usually a foreigner, asks upon discovering South Africa has eleven official languages. 'Five,' I answer: Zulu, Xhosa, Sotho, Tswana and Pedi. To tell the truth, I should say I speak six local languages, including Afrikaans, but I do not. It is an affectation, a prejudice I believe I share with millions of other black South Africans. We do not care to have it known that we are fluent in the so-called language of the oppressor. The truth is that I speak Afrikaans fairly well. I first realised this in 1993 when I became a court reporter for the *Sunday Times*. There were still only two official languages then, English and Afrikaans, and many of the cases I covered at the time were in Afrikaans. *U agbare* (Your honour), *moord* (murder), *poging tot moord* (attempted murder), *huisbraak* (housebreaking), *stilte in die hof* (silence in court): these were words and expressions I found I knew only too well during my year as a court reporter. It did not take me long to understand that I knew and spoke more Afrikaans than I cared to admit.

How could it be otherwise? Afrikaans was all around me when I was growing up. It was the language of power; the language that gave words such as *swartes* (blacks), *kleurling* (coloured), *net blankes* (whites only) and *geen ingang* (no entry) their menace. Afrikaans was also the language that gave the world 'apartheid': a word that has so seared itself into the global imagination that it requires no translation. But that is not all there was to Afrikaans. It was also the grammar for the *tsotsitaal* I heard spoken by older boys on the street; the syntax at the heart of adult conversation from which children in my house were excluded. What's more, Afrikaans was the language of Gerhardus Christiaan Coetzee, the boxing hero whose very name was as Afrikaans as a name could ever be.

I took Afrikaans as a subject all through high school and for the better part of primary school. I studied Afrikaans literature with the lazy enthusiasm of a student who needed to master something to pass, and learnt to enjoy the works of Afrikaans writers such as André Brink, Antjie Krog, Breyten Breytenbach, C.J. Langenhoven, Eugène Marais and Ingrid Jonker. But that was school Afrikaans. It was the Afrikaans I needed to make it through school and to move to the next grade. Being at a school where pupils could choose any languages they wanted, provided they were English and Afrikaans, I did not have much choice except to learn the language. Learn it I did. I made sure I knew how to handle the double negatives, how to roll my tongue so the sounds would come out just right. But I left high school with none of the confidence to claim that I was fluent in Afrikaans.

I had studied the language for longer than I would have liked.

Still, I would not say I could speak it. I also felt for Afrikaans the disdain that was a badge of honour among the wannabe revolutionaries of my high school years. It was, after all, the guttural language of orders and insults; of Bantu education, the language that had had children up in arms in 1976 as they took to the street to protest against being forced to learn everything from mathematics to science in Afrikaans. It did not help the political cause of Afrikaans among black South Africans that it was the language through which they were supposed to learn that there were stations in life above which they could not rise. So black folks had every reason to hate Afrikaans and not want to speak it or admit to speaking it.

Truth be told, the relationship between black people and Afrikaans was always more complicated than this. There were many more black people fluent in Afrikaans than were fluent in English. Recall the graffiti that appeared on the walls of Sophiatown on the eve of its destruction: 'Ons phola hier' (We are staying put). The use of Afrikaans in that statement of defiance was not a coincidence. There are black folks for whom Afrikaans rolls off the tongue a lot easier than does English. It is the language in which old men rib each other: 'Jy's nog a laaitie!' (You're still a kid!); the language in which one's provenance is established: 'Wie se laaitie is jy?' (Whose son are you?) Then there is, of course, *tsotsitaal*, the language of hipness, jazz and urban blacks. It is the language we still speak to this day. 'Dis kak maar dis alright,' we say. (Everything is OK.)

Afrikaans is also the language in which most colloquial expressions are given form. Black South Africans will say,

'Ag shame, what a beautiful baby!' when a baby is born; 'Ag shame, poor thing!' when that baby falls and hurts itself; and 'Ag shame, what a shame!' when that baby dies. It is not so much the word 'shame', which South Africans lather on to many sentences with the abandon that Americans usually reserve for ketchup, as the word 'ag' that does all the work here. This word, as guttural as any you will find in Afrikaans, does not have much meaning by itself. It is, rather, a verbal exclamation mark that takes its meaning from the context in which it is used. 'Ag nee' (Oh no), we say, when things do not go the way we want. That is 'ag'. But it is by no means the only Afrikaans colloquial expression that long ago escaped its origins. There is 'tog', an omnibus word that is part of the Katlehong argot. 'Tog' gains in potency when used alongside 'ag'. 'Tog' is used to express everything from pity to impatience or to give descriptions of a job or ritual ceremonies. You say, 'Ag tog!' when a baby falls and hurts herself; 'Ag tog!' when a neighbour fails to return your gardening tools on the appointed day; 'Ngizitholele itogwana izolo' (I found a part-time job yesterday); or 'Sizobe sinetogo kusasa' (We are hosting a little ceremony for the ancestors tomorrow).

But Afrikaans was not just a language of the street, spoken by clevers and old–timers; not just *tsotsitaal*. It was also, for me, the language of the adults in my life. Afrikaans was the language my mother spoke with her sisters, friends and neighbours when they did not want children to listen in to their adult conversations. This was back in the days when *kinders* were, well, kids.

My cousins and I knew to make ourselves scarce when

The Language of Nostalgia

my mother and her friends started speaking Afrikaans. Once, during a weekend visit to my Grandma Tala's house, my cousin Lucky and I were caught making out with the girls from next door. It was Lucky's idea. He was a good ten years older than me. But the only difference his age made when we were caught was that he got a worse pasting than I did. My weekend visit was curtailed and I was shipped straight home shortly after my beating.

I did not say anything to my mother about why I had returned home early. Instead I mumbled something when she asked and prayed that Grandma Tala would not come to visit soon. My prayers were not answered: Grandma Tala came the very next week. I could have gone out to play with my friends and disappeared into the streets, to return later after she had left, but I was not one to delay punishment. So I hung about the yard, waiting for Grandma Tala to tell my mother what had brought me home early the previous weekend and for my mother to go after me. I waited and waited. Then Grandma Tala started speaking Afrikaans. I stiffened. There was nothing to do except wait for the slippers to fly and the smacks to rain down on me. But that did not happen. Instead, my mother greeted Grandma's tale with laughter – hearty laughter. Not understanding the language spoken and unsure what to make of my mother's laughter, I hung around a little longer, waiting for a change in mood. It did not come and the two women continued to chat away in Afrikaans over cups of tea. How, then, can I not be nostalgic for Afrikaans?

As I have said, there was more to Afrikaans than conventional political history will have us believe. It might

Native Nostalgia

have been the language of the oppressor at some level, the language of order and exclusion. But it was also the language of colloquial expressions and the mode in which my mother, her friends and siblings exercised their own form of exclusionary politics. What is more, there is a deeper sense in which Afrikaans was (and is) the language of black nostalgia. In the early 1990s, shortly after the advent of democracy, a kwaito group named Skeem, itself an Afrikaans word meaning 'team', released a hit song entitled *Waar was jy?* (Where were you?) The song was a walk down memory lane that took in all the major musical and cultural events in modern black urban South African history.

'Where were you?' asked Skeem, when Brenda Fassie was her lover's weekend special? Waar was jy when Mercy Pakela was complaining about her hot sneakers? Where were you when Yvonne Chaka Chaka's MaDlamini was brewing *umqombothi* (traditional African beer)? When Stimela, arguably the best Afropop group to come out of our country, was telling South Africans that 'we're all tributaries of this great river of pain'? When Sello Chicco Twala was saying, 'We miss you Manelow' – Manelow standing here for Mandela, whose name could still not be uttered on the airwaves controlled by the SABC? *Waar was jy?* was not so much a hit as a history lesson, a paean to some of the best music to come out of black South Africa in the 1980s. Skeem were not simply reminding us of the rich artistic work that came out even in the darkest days of apartheid. They were also locating themselves in this rich musical tradition. What's more, they were doing so in a language that was supposedly that of the oppressor.

The Language of Nostalgia

Skeem did not invent the nostalgic question 'Waar was jy?' It was the question people asked to establish how hip you were. Waar was jy when Gerrie Coetzee became the first world heavyweight champ from Africa? Waar was jy when Kaizer Chiefs' Teenage Dladla singlehandedly thrashed Orlando Pirates with regular abandon in the 1980s or when Ace Mnini of Moroka Swallows dribbled his way from one side of the field to the other? Waar was jy when Patson Kamuzu Banda stood all too often between Pirates and yet another defeat? Or when Samora Khulu of the African Wanderers destroyed Kaizer Chiefs so often that Chiefs ended up buying him? Or when Dangerous Darkies roamed South Africa's premier soccer league and Jacob 'Dancing Shoes' Morake was waltzing his way through boxing rings.

'Waar was jy?' was also the question on the lips of adults, my uncles and older cousins especially, as they closed their eyes and tapped their feet to John Coltrane, Miles Davis, Dizzy Gillespie or Basil Manenberg Coetzee, Dollar Brand, Winston Mankunku Ngozi and Kippie Moeketsi. 'Waar was jy?' they would ask each other. The question was rhetorical. Turning to us young 'uns, they would sometimes mutter: 'Sonny, jy ken niks' (Boy, you know nothing). It was true: we were too young to know anything about *A Love Supreme* and *A Kind of Blue*. We knew nothing of the music that was admired in silence and praised in Afrikaans.

'Hoor net daar!' (Just listen to that), an uncle would say as a note 'slaat hom diep in die binnekant' (hit him deep in his insides). Another uncle would look into the sky, tap his shiny Florsheim shoes on the floor and then say: 'Hoor net daar.' It was understood that the expression did not require elaboration. It said everything there was to be said at the time. This is how jazz was supposed to work. More than that, this is where the music was supposed to be felt, deep in your *binnekant*, your insides.

The Istanbul of Orhan Pamuk might have its *hüzün*, that profound feeling of melancholy that marks this beautiful ugly city on two continents. South Africans on the whole do not have a word as succinct or as apt to describe our groping in the dark for the meaning of our past. We do not even have a word that sums up our longing for a home that was or never was. But we do have Afrikaans. We have 'Waar was jy?' We have 'Hoor net daar!' We speak of things that happened in the past as things that happened 'van toeka af' (long ago, back then, in the olden days). I can't say why Afrikaans should be the language of nostalgia. I can't say I know why, of South Africa's eleven official languages, Afrikaans should be the one in which our nostalgia, our *hüzün*, is expressed. Could it be that, in using Afrikaans to express our deep longing for the past, for the homes we have lost or might have lost, black South Africans might be forcing Afrikaans to speak of its origins in the kitchens or the slave quarters in the Cape? As a rule, I prefer not to speak Afrikaans with white South Africans. I find the exchange often carries too much baggage, too many unstated assumptions, too much history. So I don't know if 'Waar was jy?' is also the question of choice for white nostalgics. I don't know if Afrikaans folk music and the *tiekiedraai* allow for the kind of feet-tapping that must follow the expression 'Hoor net daar'. Do Afrikaners also close their eyes, tap their feet and ask

The Language of Nostalgia

their companions to 'Hoor net daar'? Or do they have other terms for their nostalgic musings?

Svetlana Boym says that Russians are fond of saying that the past is more unpredictable than the future. Pieter-Dirk Uys, the satirist, likes to joke that the future is the only thing about which South Africans are certain: it is the past we are not sure about. What indeed was the past to us? Was it the spectacular brutality of the askari Joe Mamasela and his bloodlust? Was it the venality of Mamasela's bosses in apartheid's death squads, Dirk Coetzee and Eugene de Kock? What indeed was apartheid to us? Was it the colonial wars of conquest – land dispossession – the migrant labour system – the influx controls and the pass system? Was it grand and petty apartheid? What indeed was it? And what of the struggle against apartheid? Was it the heroism and courage of Nelson Mandela? Or was it the pragmatism (collaborationism?) of Mandela and his Robben Island comrades? Was it resistance or collaboration? Was it both?

In 2000 I spent a year as an exchange student at a liberal arts college in Upstate New York. In my cohort were other exchange students from the Czech Republic, Romania, Hungary, Estonia, Poland and the Russian Federation. They were old enough to have lived through the dying days of Soviet communism but also young enough to have enjoyed the onset of freedom. They spoke many languages but had Russian in common – except none of them (bar the two from Russia) would speak Russian with one another. In fact, they refused to speak Russian. They loathed the language. They were more fluent in Russian than they were in English but they would

Native Nostalgia

not speak it. 'Why?' I asked once. 'Why make your lives so difficult when you could communicate easily in the language you all had in common?'

Russian was the language of their former Soviet oppressors. It was the language they had been forced to learn at school. But what about Akhmatova, Gogol, Solzhenitsyn, Turgenev, Tolstoy? What about the best of Russian music and culture? What about the Bolshoi? They did not care. They wanted nothing to do with the language of their erstwhile occupiers, they said. There were times when I thought I could understand and even sympathise with them because of my ambivalent attitude to Afrikaans. The truth is that I do not loathe Afrikaans. How could I hate a language that my mother and her siblings spoke without apology? How could I turn my back on a language that was such a big part of how I thought about the past? While I always get defensive when a white South African presumes to speak to me in Afrikaans, I do not hate the language. 'Hoor net daar,' I hear myself mutter when I listen to Miles Davis play *Prayer*. 'Waar was jy?' I ask when I hear the best of Brenda Fassie.

To say that Afrikaans is the language of black nostalgia par excellence is to strip Afrikaans of its racialised baggage. It is to say there are many more ways of resisting the depredations of power. Although the forked tongue was not designed for Afrikaans, it sure articulated it. Black South Africans could use Afrikaans without necessarily subscribing to the white supremacist ideology of those who claimed Afrikaans, despite history, as a white man's language. Listen to Noni Jabavu, one of the last of the black Victorians, describe how her father,

The Language of Nostalgia

Professor D.D.T. Jabavu, used Afrikaans to flatter and cajole his Afrikaner contemporaries. Jabavu was one of the most educated men in early twentieth-century South Africa. He taught Latin at the University of Fort Hare. Yet he was not above calling white men less educated than him 'baas'. Pity the 'baas' who thought he was indeed baas.

Then there is the account of the life of the sharecropper Kas Maine given by Charles van Onselen. Maine might not have had the support of the state behind him or the political and economic support enjoyed by his white partners and overlords. But the seed was his and he was able to deal with his white overlords in ways that benefited him for longer than should have been possible for a man of his status. And he presumably did a fair bit of his negotiating in Afrikaans. As someone once said, human beings might not choose the circumstances under which they make history, but they still make history anyway. That, I believe, is the story of black nostalgia; the story of black South Africans and their relationship to Afrikaans.

I should of course be careful not to paint my canvas with very broad brushstrokes. After all, Afrikaans does not exist in large parts of what is today KwaZulu-Natal in the same way that it exists in places such as Gauteng, Free State, North West and, of course, Limpopo. I do not know what people in KwaZulu-Natal would say to our 'Waar was jy?' or our 'Hoor net daar'. Would they respond the same way as a native of Katlehong, for example? Would they hear in those two expressions a cue to go down memory lane? I do not mean to suggest that black South Africans appropriated Afrikaans all in the same way or even that they learnt it the same way. Only a master narrative of homogeneous black suffering would peddle such a lie. As my story about blacks and apartheid shows, there were many things wrong about Bantu education. Afrikaans was one of them but it was by no means the only one. That is why black South Africans continue to speak it to this day.

Ask my brother N how he's doing: 'Kak's maar dis alright' (Crap but OK). He means 'same shit different day', 'daar's altyd kak', there's always shit to wade through, but that it's alright. In the end, 'Alles sal reg wees' (It will all be OK in the end). In my brother's earthy Afrikaans, I hear the voice of a small-time trader, which is what he is, willing it all to be alright but knowing also that it's hard being a small-time businessman. Then there is that quirk of South African township speech: the double use of a word for emphasis. Just as South Africans use the word 'actually' often and liberally, so with the Afrikaans equivalent 'eintlik'. 'Eintlik, maar Joe, wat is jou probleem?' The sentence is constructed with little or no respect for the rules of Afrikaans grammar, but its meaning is unmistakable: 'Joe, what is actually your problem? What's up?' Except we don't just use the word 'eintlik' once. You have to use it twice, 'Eintlik, eintlik …' for people to know that, actually, you mean business, that you are 'see-rius'. Though not as serious as the charge levelled at townships by the writer Denis Hirson.

Hirson writes, '"Location" and "township", like those other terms of apartheid designating places where the lives of blacks were regimented to suit white needs, such as the "Bantustan" or sweetly cynical "homeland", the "resettlement area" and "closer-settlement camp", all referred to politically

The Language of Nostalgia

frozen zones; amputated portions of the country laid down in the dust of no man's land.' Eish, maar Hirson. Where are my uncles, the township clevers with their tapping Florsheim shoes, Brentwood trousers and Viyella shirts? Where in this politically frozen zone, this amputated portion of the country, are the men and women who would 'witty' (chat) in Afrikaans, because they felt like it and liked Afrikaans? Not because white supremacists told them to like the language. If townships and locations were politically frozen zones, what did that make those black lives: politically frigid? What did that make the men and women who peopled my world and taught me the difference between right and wrong? Why would I be nostalgic for such a barren, lifeless place?

Township; location – 'lokasie' in Afrikaans; 'kasie' in township lingo. Hirson is not alone in thinking about townships in such stultifying and ultimately ahistorical terms. There always was and always will be more to townships than the designs of South Africa's political rulers. The apartheid government and its segregationist predecessors might have conceived of townships as nothing more than warehouses for labour. But townships were always more than that. They were also the places from which emerged the New Africans and their literature, even if some of that literature lamented the corrupting influence of the city and hankered after a pastoral Africa. They were the places where newly urbanised Africans adopted new musical instruments found in the city – such as the harmonica, concertina, bass guitar – and made them speak indigenous languages, including Afrikaans.

Growing up, I could never understand why township folks

Native Nostalgia

considered 'Boesman guitar' the height of insult against a coloured person. It was what children shouted at coloured people walking or travelling through Katlehong. I understood the connection between 'Boesman' and 'guitar' only much later when I learnt that coloured performers were among the first artists to adopt these new musical instruments and make them their own. Coloured performers would travel round the country, performing at shebeens and other places of supposed easy virtue. I do not know when this expertise turned into a source of insults against coloured people.

But don't think that young coloured folk took any of this 'Boesman guitar' stuff lying down. There was, I believe, only one petrol station in the Katlehong area when my brother N was growing up in the 1960s. The station was on the border between Katlehong and Thokoza, the township to the west of Katlehong, and in a section of Thokoza that housed a few coloured communities. This was apparently before the coloured families were moved to Eden Park, a coloured township to the south of both Katlehong and Thokoza. My brother says that he and his friends would run the gauntlet of bricks and slurs such as 'kaffirs' as they dashed into the petrol station, bought petrol in containers and, using sticks and stones, fought their way out of the coloured neighbourhood. It was what young people did. Did they know they were being silly and small-minded? I doubt it. For them, it was all about turf war and group warfare, about defending your 'kasie' and your 'skeem'. It was about showing the other side who was 'baas'. Tell these young men that theirs were politically frozen zones, amputated portions of the country and they would likely look at you as if

The Language of Nostalgia

'jy was heeltemal mal' (absolutely crazy in the head).

African and coloured boys were not the only ones who found in Afrikaans words ('Boesman guitar' and 'kaffir') swear words with just the right kind of venom. There were also adults who found in Afrikaans words such as *vuilpop*. The best translation I can think of is 'dirty little scoundrel'. You were a *vuilpop* if you acted in ways considered uncouth by adults. *Vuilpop* was the put-down of choice for my mother. *Vuilpops* were the worst of the worst. They were the kids who lived in a rubbish dump called Dima Paint on the northern edge of Katlehong, living off rats and goodness knows what else. *Vuilpops* were the kids who came from homes that were not quite up to the standards and expectations of the neighbourhood. So it's not difficult to see why *vuilpop* was the last thing you wanted to be, especially close to Christmas time when it was time for new clothes.

Then there was *straatmeisie* (street girl). On the face of it, *straatmeisie* referred to a prostitute, a whore (*iseqamgwaqo* in Zulu). It was the worst insult you could hurl at a woman in our neighbourhood. In truth and as is the case with such insults, *straatmeisie* was used to call into question the worth of any woman who dared to be different. *Straatmeisie* was also the word people on the street used to settle scores. I grew up right next door to a shebeen run entirely by women, and *straatmeisie* was a term I heard often in my childhood as women called to collect their spendthrift husbands, boyfriends and live-in lovers. For some reason, it was considered the fault of the women running the shebeen that husbands, fathers and boyfriends were drinking away their pay packets.

There were also expressions that one picked up as one

Native Nostalgia

discovered girls. We would walk in groups around our section, looking for girls to chat up. If we saw girls in the distance, we would wonder aloud if they were *mooi van ver* (beautiful from afar) or *ver van mooi* (far from beautiful). There was only one way to know which was which and that was to get closer to the girls concerned. I don't which questions girls asked themselves about us boys but I am certain they were not too far from our own.

These, then, are just some of the ways in which Afrikaans was a language of the townships: words, expressions, idioms, jokes that drew from Afrikaans but spoke of worlds far removed from the world of those who insisted Afrikaans was white. It is precisely because Afrikaans existed beyond the narrow confines of those who insisted on labelling it white that folks in my neighbourhood and other areas could use it to speak fondly of the past. This is not to say that the language does not bear scars from the straitjacket in which it was put. Some years ago, someone called my mobile phone number. 'Hello,' I answered. 'Wie praat?' asked a man with a thick Afrikaans accent. ('Who's speaking?' he wanted to know.) 'Jacob,' I replied. 'Ag nee,' said the man. 'Dis 'n swart man' (Oh no, it's a black man), he said and cut off the call. It was a wrong number.

8
Conclusion

When Bronislaw Malinowski visited South Africa in the 1930s, he recoiled at the sight of Africans living in cities. In the words of James Ferguson, Malinowski saw the urban African as a 'kind of frightening, pathological monstrosity'. In fact, the term 'urban African' would have been an oxymoron to Malinowski. According to Malinowski, 'the "detribalised household" of the urban African had abandoned the functional arrangements of the "tribal household" without achieving the material requirements and hygienic standards of the properly European one'. In short, the urban African lived in a world of disease and disorder. According to Ferguson, Malinowski and thinkers such as Karl Polanyi found urban Africans a problem because they disrupted the orderly divisions on which colonial planning and Western social science were founded: traditional versus modern, Western versus native. These thinkers refused to accept that one could be urban and African at the same time. Africans only made sense to them when in their world of timeless traditions. They would not accept that a native could be, well, native to a city.

It is against the backdrop of this refusal that the title of this book, *Native Nostalgia*, is to be understood. The word 'native' carries two meanings here. On the one hand, it is used in its literal sense to mean indigenous. On the other, it is used in the way it was used in colonial and segregationist times to refer to a person of African descent. The nostalgia in question also works in two ways. On one level, it refers in a conventional sense to a homesickness, a longing for a lost home. However, my nostalgia is not experienced in the ether. It is felt in a specific time and place in South African history. By insisting on my native nostalgia, I challenge claims made by Malinowski and Polanyi that to be urban and African at the same time is to be, as Ferguson describes it, an 'out of category native'.

However, my challenge is not driven by the need to prove that Zulus, too, can be urban. As the previous pages show, I take it for granted that Africans can be both native and urban. I also take it for granted that there is nothing wrong with native nostalgia, a longing for a lost home set in a politically problematic space and time. I take it as given that township natives can and do have fond memories of the places in which they were born and grew up. My memories of my childhood in Katlehong and the social orders and bonds of solidarity that animated life in the township are not intended to compensate for a life of lack. They are not some make-believe about a world that never was. They constitute instead an attempt to seize hold of memories without which we cannot understand why apartheid suffered the kind of moral defeat that led to its demise.

Conclusion

If, at one level, my nostalgia is a response to Malinowski and Polanyi, at another it is a meditation on a time seemingly out of joint – a time when black South Africans have been turned into abstract entities called PDIs (previously disadvantaged individuals) and townships have been reduced to places in need of service delivery. By setting forth my memories of the township in which I grew up, I have tried to expose the shallowness of these depictions of townships and those who people them. I have also tried to upset narratives of townships as 'sites of struggle' that have become 'sites for development'. I have done this because I believe that while places such as Katlehong have a worldliness about them that locates them in multiple elsewheres, they also display particularities of place that cannot be wished away.

As Edward Casey shows, there is a sharp distinction between place and site. Place depends on its varied production across time for its existence. Echoing Aristotle, Casey says that place 'possesses distinct potencies' that cannot be homogenised. Each place is unique. Each place is a container of memories and these are what give it its distinct potencies. Site, on the other hand, is empty. Casey says: 'A site is not a container but an open area that is specified primarily by means of cartographic representations such as maps or architects' plans. It embodies a spatiality that is at once homogeneous (i.e. having no internal differentiations with respect to material constitution) and isotropic (possessing no inherent directionality such as up/down, East/West, etc.).'

It is not difficult to understand why it was common in anti-apartheid parlance to speak of townships, factories and schools as 'sites of struggle'. This was where the struggle was fought. These so-called terrains were different places with different histories and were peopled by different individuals at different times. Calling them 'sites of struggle' allowed the liberation movement to suppress local, regional and other differences by focusing on what ostensibly united every corner of South Africa. Labelling places that were different in composition and history 'sites of struggle' allowed the liberation movement to project its vision of a post-apartheid South Africa on to 'sites' that were there, ready for new construction once apartheid was defeated. It is, after all, no coincidence that 'site' is the term given to greenfield construction, housing and other developments.

As Casey says: 'A site possesses no points of attachment onto which to hang our memories, much less to retrieve them. By denuding itself of particularity, site deprives itself of … the most efficacious cues for remembering. Place, in contrast, characteristically presents us with a plethora of such cues. Thanks to its "distinct potencies", a place is at once internally diversified – full of protuberant features and forceful vectors – and distinct externally from other places. Both kinds of differentiation, internal and external, augment memorability.' By looking at Katlehong as a place filled with embodied memories, I have provided, I hope, an appreciation of the township that fuses the anecdotal and the general without losing sight of either. I also hope that, by taking Katlehong as a particular place within a larger constellation, I have made possible a better appreciation of what makes the place different from the next township. Place provides fertile ground for

Conclusion

embodied agency and the possibility for emancipatory politics – the kind of community politics, in fact, that resulted in the defeat of apartheid.

Casey says that not only does place encourage distinctiveness, it is also there to be entered and re-entered 'by memory if not by direct bodily movement'. He continues: 'Unlike site and time, memory does not thrive on the indifferently dispersed. It thrives, rather, on the persistent particularities of what is properly in place: held fast there and made one's own.' In a move that recalls Freud's observation about Rome being a layer of memories, Casey says 'places are *congealed scenes* [his emphasis] for remembered contents; and as such they serve to situate what we remember.' It is these congealed scenes and fragments that I have examined in the previous chapters. By peeling them apart one by one, I have tried, in the manner of a reluctant tour guide, to point out the 'protuberant features and forceful vectors' that make Katlehong what it is.

However, I have not simply been an unengaged tour guide, taking the reader through the ghetto and offering nothing but descriptions with no depth. All along, I have been guided by the question of what it means for me to remember my childhood under apartheid with fondness. I have examined aspects of my childhood and brought out features of South Africa's urban history that have, I hope, made it possible for the reader to understand why there are black South Africans with fond memories of their lives under apartheid and why, fifteen years since the end of apartheid, we have blacks who 'sleep in suburbs but live in townships'. The weekly display of nostalgia by blacks paying ridiculous mortgages for houses they only sleep in but hardly ever use is not simply a case of there being no associational life in the formerly white suburbs (there is) or of whites being unwelcoming to their new black neighbours. It is rather a tacit admission that there is more to townships than their portrayals as places of crime, squalor and disease – hopeless places awaiting development by a benevolent government.

In the Introduction, I considered the memories that some black South Africans have of their past under apartheid and introduced the concept of nostalgia. By describing these memories as nostalgia, I wanted to show that memories that people have – about law and order, about a time when the word of an adult was law – have been driven by anxiety about what has gone on in post-apartheid South Africa. I wanted to show that the world of apartheid was not simply black and white, with resisters on one hand and oppressors on the other. It was a world of moral ambivalence and ambiguity in which some people could be both resisters and collaborators at the same time. By placing nostalgia at the centre of my consideration of the past, I have also sought to challenge a master narrative of black dispossession that masks deep class, ethnic and gendered fissures within black communities. Through this challenge, I have expressed my own anxiety about the political entrepreneurship and racial nativism I see all about us today as black South Africans with no history of struggle take advantage of the valorisation (or is it a fetishism?) of blackness to enrich themselves or gain positions.

In Chapter 1, I have, through a brief excursion into the biographical, looked at the place of radio and television in

Conclusion

a township home in the 1970s and 1980s. By examining the place of radio, a propaganda tool of the apartheid regime, in my childhood, I have illustrated the ways in which the world of apartheid was in effect a world of grey zones. In this world, it was not unthinkable for black families to back a white (African) boxer against a black (American) fighter. It was also not odd for black South Africans to enjoy Radio Zulu without at the same time buying into the chauvinist politics which the station tried to promote. Radio gave its black listeners a freedom of movement denied them by influx control and its pass laws. It also created an imagined community of listeners that cut across ethnicity and regional differences.

In Chapter 2, I have approached Katlehong from the air, as it were, all along keen to point out the gap between the way the place looks on paper and the way it looks in reality; the way government 'reads' it and the way those who inhabit its streets experience it. By pointing out this gap, I have sought to challenge the economistic conceptions of townships as warehouses for labour and little else. The township may have been founded to house Africans who would service white needs, but it escaped that straitjacket the moment the first brick was laid and the first shack erected. But I have not simply laid out the moment of Katlehong's founding. I have also extended it to show that the township exists in the world.

The township is a world in flux, forever changing. In Chapter 3, I have considered one of the most visible manifestations of these changes: the rat epidemic that has hit every South African township. The epidemic has become a source of anxiety as communities feel overwhelmed by these visitors from

Native Nostalgia

below. From tabloids to focus groups, street conversations to nightmares, the rat has become the symbol par excellence of a time out of joint. One needs to be in a township at night, when rats come out to play, to see that townships may have become like Theodora, one of the hidden cities in Italo Calvino's *Invisible Cities*. For centuries Theodora has been subjected to recurrent invasion – by serpents, spiders, flies, termites, woodworms – but each time the residents have managed to rout the enemy. Calvino writes: 'But first, for many long years, it was uncertain whether or not the final victory would not go to the last species left to fight man's possession of the city: the rats.' In Theodora, the rat epidemic was only controlled when 'At last, with an extreme massacre, the murderous, versatile ingenuity of mankind defeated the overweening life force of the enemy'. But this is not about to happen in South African townships. If anything, rats are strangers in our midst come to remind us that Gauteng, the place of gold, owes its existence to the subterranean.

In Chapter 4, I have examined social distinction within black schools and neighbourhoods. I have shown the ways in which these distinctions were 'performed' at school as our teachers used music to try to 'improve' us working-class kids in the same way presumably that the modern black elite, which owes its existence to missionary churches and their schools, was originally 'improved' by white missionaries. I have also examined the ways in which ideas of hygiene and contamination were used to mark out and quarantine those of us who grew up in townships. The main concern here has been to show that the 'masses of our people' of struggle lore were

Conclusion

not one undifferentiated mass but a collection of individuals from different class, ethnic and gendered backgrounds. I have also been keen to challenge the myth of the 'black middle-class role model'. The black working class had its own role models.

In Chapter 5, I have examined some of the social orders and displays of social capital that animated my childhood and the worlds of the adults in my life. Using the way in which money was parcelled out and bereaved families succoured, I have tried to show that there were more instances of solidarity than conventional struggle history would have us believe. By doing this, I have, I hope, shown that there were practices of everyday life in townships that fed into people's imaginings of a better world. This is not to valorise these practices or to see in every township practice an act of resistance. Rather, it is to point out that there was always more to township life than *sukkeling*, struggle.

In Chapter 6, I have foregrounded one of the key impulses of the book, namely the idea that townships are places of the senses. I have made the argument that a township is a world of the senses that can and does work on one's nerves. The idea here is to show that townships are not dead zones, spaces without feeling. The people who inhabit townships see, smell, taste, touch and hear. They cannot do otherwise. It is important to remind ourselves of this because the tendency is to focus on only a few ways in which townships can get on one's nerves (the pollution, the noise, disease, etc.) and neglect the fact that, here too, people use every sense available to them to live. But I have not left it there. I have also looked at the ways in which even in those episodes for which Katlehong is notorious, such as the violence that nearly derailed South Africa's transition to democracy, the senses played a key part: from residents complaining about the smelly armpits of taxi drivers to apartheid town planners saying sewerage works for black were more expensive because blacks were too full of shit.

In Chapter 7, I have proposed what is to my mind a delicious conundrum, namely that Afrikaans is the language of black nostalgia. I have recalled colloquial Afrikaans expressions and idioms that are part of the Katlehong argot. I have also pointed out the fact that for me while growing up, Afrikaans was the language of adult conversation. By bringing this to the fore, I hope I have undermined some of the claims that portray the relationship between black South Africans and Afrikaans as always having been hostile. The students who took to the streets in 1976 to protest against the use of Afrikaans as a medium of instruction carried placards that read 'Down with Apartheid'. But there were many more blacks who spoke Afrikaans and did so with pride. This is not to say that they supported apartheid or the ends to which the language was put by the apartheid state.

As the book has shown, the township is no stranger to thought. It has lent its name to a popular movement called township art, inspired musical genres such as township jazz and kwaito, and served as both narrative backdrop and creative source for black writers working in English and indigenous languages. The township was also the metaphorical black home in whose living room the post-apartheid imaginary was largely conceived by a revolutionary movement that never

Conclusion

really moved out of its urban base, despite agrarian pretensions best exemplified by anti-apartheid slogans such as 'Mayibuy' iAfrika' and 'Izwe Lethu', that placed the return of 'the land' to indigenous Africans at the centre of the fight for freedom. The anti-apartheid ranks were, of course, not the only place where the township was thought about and theorised.

As is shown by the example of apartheid town planners fretting over costly sewerage works for blacks, the township was as much a challenge for the white state. However, whereas for the pro-democracy movement the township was largely the model of what post-apartheid South Africa should *not* look like, for the apartheid state the 'problem' oscillated between effecting political control, on the one hand, and ensuring that townships served the needs of industry as dormitories for labour, on the other. Apartheid planners had to find ways to keep townships under control and at the same time to 'develop' townships at cost but sufficiently for people to live there. The planners had to do all this while working, especially for the first three decades of apartheid rule, towards the ultimate Verwoerdian goal of removing blacks from 'white' South Africa. This was an apartheid illusion, to be sure, but no less real for that.

The apartheid state is no more, but townships are still with us. In fact, townships and the informal settlements that have emerged on their margins have assumed greater importance in the geography of post-apartheid South Africa as the South African population has become majority urban. However – and ironically for a place that continues to be considered by many to be barren and desolate – the township still provides fecund ground for artists and writers in the new South Africa. From the famed clothing label Stoned Cherrie, whose name and clothes draw on a deep well of nostalgia for the township of the 1950s, and the singer-songwriter Simphiwe Dana, whose sounds echo those of the songstresses of the 1950s, to writers such as Fred Khumalo and Eric Miyeni, whose musings on the new South Africa are grounded in the reality of the township, the township has inspired them in one way or another. Their work is still informed by its multiple realities and seized with its meaning.

Naturally, not all those who have given thought to the township over the years have done so in the same way. Many even have tended to define the township in negative terms. They have tended to see it as a zone of lack and deprivation. Miyeni even goes so far as to equate townships to sewers while Dana calls them places of madness. Miyeni is in many ways a paradigmatic example of the tendency to denigrate townships. He describes them as an 'unnatural environment' and compares township residents to flies trapped in a jar. He writes: 'The hardest thing anyone can do is swim out of a sewer. For one thing, the oxygen supply is limited and oxygen is a large source of the energy that that person will need to swim the length of the sewer in the first place. And so a lot of us suffocate and die, long before we can see the end of the filthy tunnel. What is worrying though is that a large number of us don't even try to swim out. Instead, we assume the sewer is our lot.'

Miyeni says that 'townships are elevated to levels way above their station' and that 'progress is limited' there. He

Conclusion

continues: 'We fought apartheid so that all of South Africa can be a home to all South Africans. The jar is now open. We must not settle down and believe that because the townships are the places where we were born, we must make our homes there. We are built for bigger and better lives, Mandingo, and we can achieve those now. Let's do it.'

This raises the question: If we fought to make all of South Africa a home to all South Africans, where then do townships belong? Are they in a different country? Do townships not occupy the same space–time configuration as the rest of South Africa? In my view Miyeni is engaging in a warped construction of townships that sees them as located in the 'there and then' of some chaotic and undefined past that should have disappeared with apartheid. He wants us to move to formerly white suburbs, which are in the 'here and now' of modernity. He says: 'Let's work to get our people to a point where they can afford to leave places like Soweto and settle in places like Melville and Sandton ... Let's work to be economically free to live anywhere we choose to live in South Africa, Mandingo.'

However, townships are not going anywhere, Mandingo. In ending with Miyeni, we have come full circle from Malinowski and Polanyi. This book will have succeeded if it helps the reader realise that a lot of what passes for common sense about townships is in fact cant. It will have succeeded if it helps the reader come to a new sense of townships and their place in the historical, political and cultural geography of South Africa. It is only by understanding that geography that we can understand why blacks would remember their past under apartheid with fondness. There is no other way.

References

Introduction

Arendt, Hannah, *Responsibility and Judgment*, New York: Schocken, 2005

Bonner, Philip and Noor Nieftagodien, *Kathorus: A History*, Cape Town: Maskew Miller Longman, 2001

Boym, Svetlana, *The Future of Nostalgia*, New York: Basic Books, 2001

Moore Jr, Barrington, *Injustice: The Social Bases of Obedience and Revolt*, London: Macmillan, 1978

Davis, Fred, *Searching for Yesterday: A Sociology of Nostalgia*, New York: Free Press, 1979

Krog, Antjie, *Country of My Skull*, Johannesburg: Random House, 1998

Nkosi, Lewis, *Home and Exile*, London: Longman, 1965

Perry, Alex, 'Why South Africa's over the Rainbow', *Time*, 20 April 2009

Steinberg, Jonny, *Thin Blue: The Unwritten Rules of Policing South Africa*, Johannesburg: Jonathan Ball Publishers, 2008

Stewart, Susan, *On Longing: Narratives of the Miniature, the Gigantic, the Souvenir, the Collection*, Durham and London: Duke University Press, 1993

Thompson, E.P., *The Making of the English Working Class*, London: Vintage Books, 1980

Vladislavić, Ivan, *Portrait with Keys: Jo'burg and What-What*, Houghton, Umuzi, 2006

Walker, Cherryl, *Landmarked: Land Claims and Land Restitution in South Africa*, Johannesburg: Jacana Media, 2008

Chapter 1

Coplan, David, *In Township Tonight! Three Centuries of South African Black City Music and Theatre*, Johannesburg: Jacana, 2007

Gunner Liz, 'Wrestling with the Present, Beckoning to the Past: Contemporary Zulu Radio Drama', *Journal of Southern African Studies*, 26, 2, June 2000

Gunner Liz, 'Resistant Medium: The Voices of Zulu Radio Drama in the 1970s', *Theatre Research International*, 27, 3, 2002

1973, Remember When … A Nostalgic Look Back in Time, Tennessee: Seek Publishing

Chapter 2

Agamben, Giorgio, *Infancy and History: On the Destruction of Experience*, trans. by Liz Heron, London: Verso, 2007

Benjamin, Walter, *Berlin Childhood around 1900*, trans. by Howard Eiland, Cambridge, Mass.: Belknap Press of Harvard University, 2006

Benjamin, W. and Asja Lacis, 'Naples', in *Reflections: Essays, Aphorisms, Autobiographical Writings*, trans. by Edmund Jephcott and ed. by Peter Demetz, New York: Harcourt Brace Jovanovich, 1978

Bonner, Philip and Noor Nieftagodien, *Kathorus: A History*, Cape Town: Maskew Miller Longman, 2001

Brandel-Syrier, Mia, *Coming Through: The Search for a New Cultural Identity*, Johannesburg: McGraw-Hill Book Company, 1978

Brandel-Syrier, Mia, *Reeftown Elite: A Study of Social Mobility in an African Community on the Reef*, London: Routledge, 1971

Calderwood, D.M., *Native Housing in South Africa*, Dissertation for Doctor of Architecture degree at Wits University, 1953

Calvino, Italo, *Invisible Cities*, London: Vintage, 1997

Farvacque-Vitković, Catherine et al., *Street Addressing and the Management of Cities*, Washington, D.C.: The World Bank, 2005

References

Hart, Gillian, *Disabling Globalisation: Places of Power in Post-Apartheid South Africa*, Pietermaritzburg: University of Natal Press, 2002

Hughes, Robert, *Barcelona*, New York: Knopf, 1992.

Kieder, P.J., 'The Cost of Administration, Supervision and Services in Urban Bantu Townships', *CSIR Research Report*, Pretoria: CSIR, 1964

Kostof, Spiro, *The City Shaped: Urban Patterns and Meanings through History*, Boston, Mass.: Little, Brown, 1991

Pamuk, Orhan, *Istanbul: Memories and the City*, New York: Vintage Books, 2004

Massey, Doreen, *Place, Space and Gender*, Cambridge: Polity Press, 1994

Mathewson, James Edward, *The Establishment of a Bantu Township*, Pretoria: Van Schaik, 1957

Mbembe, Achille, Nsizwa Dlamini and Grace Khunou, 'Soweto Now', in *Johannesburg: The Elusive Metropolis*, ed. by Achille Mbembe and Sarah Nuttall, Johannesburg: Wits University Press, 2008

Sachs, Albie, 'Preparing Ourselves for Freedom' in *Art from South Africa*, Oxford: Museum of Modern Art, 1990

Chapter 3

De Graaff, Gerrit, *The Rodents of Southern Africa: Notes on their Identification, Distribution, Ecology, and Taxonomy*, Durban: Butterworths, 1981

Orwell, George, *Nineteen Eighty-four*, Harmondsworth: Penguin Books, 2003

Mbembe, Achille and Sarah Nuttall, 'Introduction: Afropolis', in *Johannesburg: The Elusive Metropolis*, ed. by Achille Mbembe and Sarah Nuttall, Johannesburg: Wits University Press, 2008

Chapter 4

Bourdieu, Pierre, *Distinction: A Social Critique of the Judgment of Taste*, trans. by Richard Nice, Cambridge, Mass.: Harvard University Press, 2002

Fanon, Frantz, *The Wretched of the Earth*, New York: Grove Press, 2004

Seekings, Jeremy and Nicoli Nattrass, *Class, Race, and Inequality in South Africa*, Pietermaritzburg: University of KwaZulu-Natal Press, 2006

Chapter 5

Adorno, Theodor, *Minima Moralia: Reflections on a Damaged Life*, London: Verso, 2005

Benjamin, Walter, *Illuminations*, ed. by Hannah Arendt and trans. by Harry Zohn, New York: Harcourt, Brace and World, 1968

Brandel-Syrier, Mia, *Coming Through: The Search for a New Cultural Identity*, Johannesburg: McGraw-Hill Book Company, 1978

Hart, Gillian, *Disabling Globalisation: Places of Power in Post-Apartheid South Africa*, Pietermaritzburg: University of Natal Press, 2002

Harvey, David, *Consciousness and the Urban Experience: Studies in the History and Theory of Capitalist Urbanization*, Baltimore: Johns Hopkins University Press, 1985

Huyssen, Andreas, *Present Pasts: Urban Palimpsests and the Politics of Memory*, Stanford: Stanford University Press, 2003

Lefebvre, Henri, *The Production of Space*, Cambridge, Mass.: Blackwell, 1991

Moore Jr, Barrington, *Injustice: The Social Bases of Obedience and Revolt*, London: Macmillan, 1978

Mbembe, Achille, Nsizwa Dlamini and Grace Khunou, 'Soweto Now', in *Johannesburg: The Elusive Metropolis*, ed. by Achille Mbembe and Sarah Nuttall, Johannesburg: Wits University Press, 2008

Chapter 6

Ackerman, Diane, *A Natural History of the Senses*, New York: Vintage, 1990

Killen, Andreas, *Berlin Electropolis: Shock, Nerves, and German Modernity*, Berkeley: University of California Press, 2006

Lefebvre, Henri, *The Production of Space*, Cambridge, Mass.: Blackwell, 1991

Marais, G. and R. van der Kooy, *South Africa's Urban Blacks: Problems*

References

and Challenges, Pretoria: University of South Africa, 1978

Mathewson, James Edward, *The Establishment of a Bantu Township*, Pretoria: Van Schaik, 1957

Polanyi, Karl, quoted by James Ferguson in 'Formalities of Poverty: Thinking about Social Assistance in Neoliberal South Africa', *African Studies Review*, 50, 2, September 2007

Simmel, Georg, *On Individuality and Social Forms: Selected Writings*, ed. by Donald Levine, Chicago: Chicago University Press, 1971

Chapter 7

Boym, Svetlana, *The Future of Nostalgia*, New York: Basic Books, 2001

Coplan, David, *In Township Tonight! Three Centuries of South African Black City Music and Theatre*, Johannesburg: Jacana Media, 2007

Hirson, Denis, *White Scars: On Reading and Rites of Passage*, Johannesburg: Jacana Media, 2006

Jabavu, Noni, *Drawn in Colour: African Contrasts*, London: John Murray, 1960

Pamuk, Orhan, *Istanbul: Memories and the City*, New York: Vintage, 2004

Van Onselen, Charles, *The Seed Is Mine: The Life of Kas Maine, a South African Sharecropper, 1894–1985*, New York: Hill and Wang, 1996

Conclusion

Calvino, Italo, *Invisible Cities*, London: Vintage, 1997

Casey, Edward, *Remembering: A Phenomenological Study*, Bloomington: Indiana University Press, 1987

Malinowski, Bronislaw, quoted by James Ferguson in 'Formalities of Poverty: Thinking about Social Assistance in Neoliberal South Africa', *African Studies Review*, 50, 2, September 2007

Miyeni, Eric, *O! Mandingo: The Only Black at a Dinner Party*, Johannesburg: Jacana Media, 2006